Becoming a Psychology Professor

Becoming a Psychology Professor

Your Guide to Landing the Right Academic Job

Guy A. Boysen

AMERICAN PSYCHOLOGICAL ASSOCIATION
Washington, DC

The opinions and statements published are the responsibility of the author, and such opinions and statements do not necessarily represent the policies of the American Psychological Association.

Published by
American Psychological Association
750 First Street, NE
Washington, DC 20002
https://www.apa.org

Order Department
https://www.apa.org/pubs/books
order@apa.org

In the U.K., Europe, Africa, and the Middle East, copies may be ordered from Eurospan
https://www.eurospanbookstore.com/apa
info@eurospangroup.com

Typeset in Charter by Circle Graphics, Inc., Reisterstown, MD

Printer: Sheridan Books, Chelsea, MI
Cover Designer: Gwen J. Grafft, Minneapolis, MN

Library of Congress Cataloging-in-Publication Data
Names: Boysen, Guy A., author.
Title: Becoming a psychology professor : your guide to landing the right
    academic job / Guy A. Boysen.
Description: Washington, DC : American Psychological Association, [2020] |
    Includes bibliographical references and index.
Identifiers: LCCN 2019005540 (print) | LCCN 2019007328 (ebook) |
    ISBN 9781433830631 (eBook) | ISBN 1433830639 (eBook) |
    ISBN 9781433830600 (pbk.) | ISBN 1433830604 (pbk.)
Subjects: LCSH: Psychology—Vocational guidance. | Psychology teachers. |
    Psychology—Study and teaching (Higher)
Classification: LCC BF76 (ebook) | LCC BF76 .B69 2020 (print) |
    DDC 150.76—dc23
LC record available at https://lccn.loc.gov/2019005540

http://dx.doi.org/10.1037/0000152-000

Printed in the United States of America

10 9 8 7 6 5 4 3 2 1

Contents

Becoming a Psychology Professor

INTRODUCTION

Welcome to the Profession!

So, you want to be a psychology professor! I may be biased, but I think that you have chosen a great profession. Psychology professors get to learn new things about the mind and behavior—the most fascinating topics imaginable—and then share their most interesting findings with other people, be it in the classroom or in the pages of an academic journal. For psychology professors, there is always more work to do and better ways to do it, but the cyclical nature of teaching and the cumulative nature of science provide career-long opportunities for growth and discovery.

What psychology-related skill do you want to hone for the rest of your career? Is it engaging students in the classroom? Perhaps it is brilliance in the lab? Or do you want to devote yourself to excellence in teaching *and* research? Well, the good news is that being a psychology professor allows you to emphasize the twin pillars of academic life—teaching and research— to the degree that best matches your skills and interests, at least if you can convince the right college to hire you, which is no easy feat. Thus, the purpose of this book is to help you decide what type of professor you want to be and then provide you with a framework for gathering, documenting,

http://dx.doi.org/10.1037/0000152-001
Becoming a Psychology Professor: Your Guide to Landing the Right Academic Job,
by G. A. Boysen

and communicating the set of experiences needed to get hired as that type of professor.

WHY THIS BOOK IS NECESSARY

Have you looked for a place to eat lately? I just searched online for restaurants near my suburban home and came up with 459 options. It would be absurd to leave the house hungry for pizza and think that any one of those restaurants will lead to an equally satisfying meal. Have you looked for places to work lately? There are more than 4,600 colleges in the United States (Carnegie Classification of Institutions of Higher Education, 2016), so it is also absurd to leave graduate school thinking that a job at any one of those colleges will lead to an equally satisfying career. The most important lesson in this book is becoming a psychology professor is all about fit—you, the college, and the position must all be aligned.

Finding the proper career alignment can be challenging because of the vast differences in faculty work between colleges. Consider a professor at a community college and one at a doctoral university. Each semester at a community college, the professor may be teaching half a dozen courses, advising dozens of students, and serving on multiple university committees. Down the road at a doctoral university, the professor may be teaching one small graduate seminar, advising a dissertation project, serving as a journal editor, and managing a multimillion-dollar research grant. These two jobs are not made for people with the same interests and talents. Nonetheless, students, mentors, and the writers of advice for landing academic jobs too often treat being a professor as if there is one track rather than many.

Professors come in different varieties, but advice about careers in academia almost exclusively emphasizes jobs at research-intensive institutions. The assumption is that everyone wants to be, and will become, a duplicate of their graduate school mentor. Although faculty at research-heavy doctoral universities represent a huge proportion of all psychology professors, not everyone wants to work in that setting; moreover, not everyone who wants to will get the opportunity. In fact, half of all full-time faculty work outside of doctoral universities and most faculty spend most of their time on teaching rather than research (American Association of University Professors, 2017; National Center for Educational Statistics, 1997; "The Almanac of Higher Education: 2017–18," 2017). Thus, the purpose of this book is to provide guidance for careers at all types of colleges, not just the research-intensive ones. Specifically, the book outlines the essential experiences and strategies needed to land positions at doctoral universities, master's universities, baccalaureate colleges, and community colleges.

TYPES OF FACULTY POSITIONS

One of the central themes of this book is that professors have dramatically different jobs depending on the type of college where they work. However, each type of college employs faculty members with different titles and roles, and the job of being a professor is also dramatically different depending on these variations in position. In the eyes of students, "professors" of various brands are interchangeable. In the eyes of faculty, profound distinctions exist between the rights, responsibilities, and prestige of various faculty positions. If you doubt this, ask some tenured professors if they would be willing to give up their positions to take jobs as adjuncts. Their reactions to the very premise of the question will illustrate the importance of differences in positions. Aspiring faculty should take care in selecting institutions and in selecting positions.

Tenure Track and Continuing Contract

The type of faculty position that receives the most attention, and that most people have in mind when they think about being a professor, is tenure-track. A tenure-track position means that a new faculty member is hired and then given a certain time frame, typically 6 years, to accumulate a professional record of high-enough quality to be judged by a committee of faculty as worthy of tenure. Earning tenure generally means that a faculty member no longer needs to regularly establish his or her fitness for employment, and with this status comes exceptional freedom in the self-direction of scholarship and teaching. Tenure is often accompanied by promotion to the rank of associate professor from assistant professor, and it puts faculty on the track to apply eventually for promotion to professor, which is the highest rank faculty members can achieve. Earning tenure is stressful and time-consuming, but it comes with a high reward.

Not all institutions offer tenure, but those that do not sometimes have an alternative type of continuing contract. After an initial probationary period during which faculty must undergo annual review of their work and reappointment to a full-time position, a continuing contract kicks in, and faculty are automatically hired for an additional year of work. Unlike tenure, continuing contracts have a definite endpoint, typically 5 years, after which another contract must be extended by the college. Nonetheless, continuing-contract positions offer similar job stability as tenure-track positions.

Instructor and Lecturer

Instructors and lecturers are full-time faculty who are not on the tenure track. The specific title varies between institutions, but an essential characteristic of the position is that the guarantee of work lasts only as long as specified by a contract, typically 1 school year. Compared with their tenure-track colleagues, full-time instructors spend more time teaching and less time engaged in other professional duties (Morphew, Ward, & Wolf-Wendel, 2016). In fact, some university work, such as committees related to tenure and faculty governance, may specifically exclude faculty who are not on the tenure track. Although instructors may find time in their schedules to conduct research, they should not expect it to be part of their contractual duties or to receive much support from their university for doing so. An instructor position can be a great opportunity for individuals who do not want to be tied down by a long-term responsibility to an institution or who want to focus solely on teaching, but if the goal is to eventually land a tenure-track position, working for long periods as an instructor will hinder that plan if the exclusive focus on teaching prevents the professional development, service, or scholarship required to be a competitive tenure-track candidate.

Instructors With Tenure or Continuing Contracts

There is a small but significant number of professors whose faculty role represents a hybrid of the instructor and tenure or continuing contract positions. Titles associated with such positions include teaching professor, professor of practice, and clinical professor. What the various positions have in common is that they emphasize student instruction, often to the total exclusion of research, but offer opportunities for promotion and security of employment. In other words, some institutions, mostly doctoral universities with high research expectations, have decided to reward excellent instructors with tenure-like contracts.

Visiting Professor

One of the more prevalent variations of full-time, but not tenure-track, faculty is the visiting professor. The key idea of visiting professorships is that they are, by definition, time-limited. Depending on the position, the time frame may be 1 year to 3 years, and occasionally there is an opportunity to apply for reappointment after the initial time frame concludes. There is an implicit assumption that visiting professor positions are for people in the early parts of their careers (there are some "distinguished" visiting positions for established scholars). For early-career psychologists, visiting positions represent a valuable chance to gain experience at a certain type of college before applying for tenure-track positions, or they are a fallback when a tenure-track position is not available. Overall, the operative word is *visiting*. A visiting professor must eventually move on to a more permanent position, and an extended series of visiting professorships does not make for a solid career foundation.

Adjunct

Adjuncts are non–tenure-track, part-time teachers who are paid on a per-course basis. Hiring adjuncts is a short-term scheme to save money because paying a flat rate to four adjuncts to teach four courses represents just a fraction of what it costs to hire one full-time faculty member to teach those same courses. Departments hire adjuncts to teach—nothing more. They may teach as many courses as full-time faculty (American Association of University Professors, 2014; Hurtado, Eagan, Pryor, Whang, & Tran, 2011), but they are not treated like full-time faculty members in terms of pay, benefits, support, or professional development opportunities. In one survey, 75% of adjuncts reported that they did not seek out the position by choice and would prefer to have a full-time position (Hurtado et al., 2011). Although many adjuncts see their teaching positions as a foot in the door to a full-time position, there is little reason to believe in the effectiveness of this strategy outside of institutions that are exclusively teaching-focused (Hurtado et al., 2011; Kelsky, 2015; Vick, Furlong, & Lurie, 2016). The problem faced by adjuncts in competing for full-time positions is that teaching eclipses all their other activities, and there is little chance to build up the professional record required to be an attractive hire for a full-time position.

The Default Position of This Book

One of the sobering facts about higher education is that the typical college professor is no longer on the tenure track, or even employed full time. Part-time instructors make up 40% of college teachers, 17% are full time but not tenure track, and 14% are graduate students (American Association of

University Professors, 2017). That leaves only 29% of full-time faculty who are tenured or on the tenure track.

Although tenure-track and continuing-contract professors represent a minority of the academic workforce, they serve as the default position types throughout this book. The main reason for this approach is that I believe they are the default positions in most people's minds. Think about yourself. When you set the career goal that led you to read this book, I bet you were imagining yourself as a tenure-track professor. Other types of positions can make for satisfying careers, but I think few people start off with the goal of being an instructor or an adjunct. Another reason for the default position is that graduate students may not immediately know the direction of their career path. As such, they should gather key experiences in scholarship, teaching, and service; this is the approach needed to obtain a tenure-track or continuing-contract position, and having a well-rounded professional record allows for the most flexibility when pursuing work as a professor. Aspiring faculty who are ready to compete for tenure-track and continuing-contract jobs will also be competitive for other positions.

THE JOB MARKET

Before dispensing advice for a career in academia, it is worth considering the overall health of the profession. No one wants to spend a decade or so training for a career only to find it dead on arrival. Worry not, because psychology professors are not going the way of travel agents or newspaper editors anytime soon. Starting with the overall field, being a college professor is a growing profession. There were 1,313,000 "postsecondary teaching" jobs in 2014, and this number is expected to increase by 13% before 2025 (Bureau of Labor Statistics, 2015). Psychology especially is among the top academic areas in terms of growth of full-time faculty positions (Morphew et al., 2016). Members of academic departments in some fields fear that they will be shuttered or that outgoing faculty will not be replaced, but psychology is not among them. The number of psychology majors has increased each year since the 1970s, and the number of master's and doctorate degrees awarded is increasing as well (National Center for Educational Statistics, 2017). Psychology education is in high demand.

That is the good news. The bad news is how college teaching jobs are being filled. Most college teachers are now hired on temporary contracts as adjuncts or instructors rather than on the tenure track (Desrochers & Kirshstein, 2014; Hurlburt & McGarrah, 2017). Tenure-track positions have become a rare and highly sought-after commodity. Open tenure-track positions in psychology receive about 50 applicants on average, but that number rises to triple digits for the most desirable positions (Benson & Buskist, 2005; Brems, Lampman, & Johnson, 1995; Eby, Allen, Evans, Ng, & DuBois, 2008; Gore, Murdock, & Haley, 1998; Sheehan & Haselhorst, 1999; Sheehan, McDevitt, & Ross, 1998; Troisi, Christopher, & Batsell, 2014). The next generation of psychology professors must be aware that competition for full-time positions has never been higher.

YOUR GUIDE TO SUCCESS IN THE JOB MARKET

The purpose of this book is to help aspiring professors find success on the academic job market. The first step toward success is setting the goal for what type of professor you aspire to be. To help you set that goal, Chapter 1 outlines the four major types of higher education institutions—doctoral universities, master's universities, baccalaureate colleges, and community colleges—and what it means to be a professor in each of these settings. Across institutions, research and teaching are the core components of faculty work, so Chapter 2 outlines the basic experiences all aspiring professors should have in those two areas. Although psychology departments want to hire accomplished scholars and teachers, they also want faculty who are responsible and collegial. Thus, Chapter 3 describes how service, mentorship, and networking lead to a positive professional reputation.

Who can benefit from the guidance in these chapters? If you are a graduate student who has started to think about the job-search process or if you already have a degree and are seeking to forge a new path in academia, Chapters 1 through 3 will help you assess your fit at different institutions and provide you with suggestions for increasing that fit. If you are just starting out in grad school, these first chapters will give you an understanding of different career paths in academia and help you map out the next 4 or 5 years of your professional life.

A strong curriculum vitae (CV) and a positive reputation are not enough to land a faculty job. Even the most accomplished applicants will be rejected if they apply for the wrong positions or if their applications send the wrong message. So, Chapter 4 describes the methods for finding positions and narrowing them down by fit. Chapter 5 on CVs and Chapter 6 on applications describe how to create application materials that will convince search committees that your credentials match the requirements of a position. Chapter 7 focuses on the interview process, how to prepare for it, and the ways that interviews are different by institution. Finally, Chapter 8 is about handling job offers and negotiations, which is exactly where aspiring faculty want to find themselves in the end.

Chapters 4 through 8 are most relevant to people who are actively preparing for a job search. However, I also recommend them to graduate students who are just starting to consider an academic career. Figure out now what it takes to land a faculty job and use that information to guide your professional development.

Going beyond the first eight chapters, even more resources are available in the book's Appendix, as well as on this book's companion website (http://pubs.apa.org/books/supp/boysen/). The Appendix includes a detailed timeline to help you stay organized during the months-long process of going on the academic job market. To help graduate students who are still formulating their professional plans, the website includes self-assessment tools for exploring types of institutions and checklists for key experiences related to research, teaching, service, and professional connections. To help people who are actively searching for jobs, the website contains examples of what standard application materials look like when applying for teaching- and research-focused positions. There are also checklists to help prepare for the application and interview processes.

Although this book is primarily for job seekers, my hope is that faculty who are training the next generation of psychology professors will read it as well. Faculty mentors should acknowledge that most graduate students will not become their academic clones. As such, they should be prepared to offer advice about academic careers at all types of institutions, and this book is an excellent source for that advice.

CONCLUSION

Differences between academic positions are profound. To take the most extreme example, the job of being a professor at a community college and a doctoral university just barely overlap. As such, when searching for new faculty at those institutions, the top candidates at the very best doctoral universities would not make the short list of job candidates at a community college and vice versa—fit with position matters that much. Aspiring professors take note: You would not want it any other way. The variety in positions and the diversity of qualifications needed to be successful in those positions provides you with the opportunity to become exactly the type of psychology professor you want to be. I hope this book helps you take advantage of that opportunity.

1

THE VARIETIES OF ACADEMIC EXPERIENCES

Types of Institutions

Being a psychology professor means different things to different people. A professor from a doctoral university who had devoted much of his career to fostering community-based service and research recounted to me the experience of inviting a colleague from another, nationally renowned university to give an address at a local conference. The colleague replied, "Yes, you can set it up with my agent," leading to the incredulous reply "You have an agent?" It turns out that, after publishing a successful book, the colleague's work now included traveling the country to give presentations with a standard speaking fee of $10,000. Here I was, a psychology professor at a baccalaureate college, speaking with a psychology professor from a doctoral university, and we were both dumbfounded by what a third professor had made out of his career at a different type of institution. And yet we ostensibly all had the same job. How did three psychology professors end up with such different professional roles?

The work of being a professor breaks down to scholarship, teaching, and service. *Scholarship* refers to faculty's contributions to science, primarily the publication of research. *Teaching* involves instruction of students, typically

http://dx.doi.org/10.1037/0000152-002
Becoming a Psychology Professor: Your Guide to Landing the Right Academic Job,
by G. A. Boysen

11

by delivering courses. *Service* refers to any other work that faculty contribute to keep their department, college, or profession running smoothly, such as serving on committees or taking on administrative roles. Scholarship, teaching, and service are the universal components of academic life, but the ability of faculty to pursue them differently is what makes being a professor such a richly varied profession. Yet professors are not completely free to follow their academic whims. Colleges and universities emphasize different faculty roles depending on mission, and faculty must fit their work within the boundaries of that institutional mission. Returning to the question of how psychology professors end up with different professional roles, it is largely because of where they work.

In this chapter, I provide an overview of faculty work at different types of higher education institutions to help ensure that you end up in a position that matches your professional interests and skills. The Carnegie system of basic classification offers more than 30 categorizations of colleges and universities (Carnegie Classification of Institutions of Higher Education, 2016). I offer four: doctoral universities, master's universities, baccalaureate colleges, and community colleges. Use these four types as a simplifying heuristic during career planning, professional development, and your job search. However, remember that variations within the types are extensive and that all institutions employ faculty who emphasize research, teaching, and service to differing degrees. So keep yourself open to multiple types of institutions when setting career goals.

DOCTORAL UNIVERSITIES

Doctoral universities (also known as doctorate-granting universities) have a larger impact on both psychology and the public than any other type of institution. To begin, if you want to be a psychology professor, chances are that you have been enrolled in one of these institutions because that is where new PhDs are minted. The size of doctoral universities also makes them influential. Although they are the least common type of college with about 330 institutions in the United States, they enroll about 6.5 million students— that is almost 20,000 per campus (Carnegie Classification of Institutions of Higher Education, 2016). Generalizations aside, doctoral universities are not monolithic. Consider Rice University and Arizona State University: They are, respectively, private and public, small and large, and highly selective and not as selective. What holds them together as an overarching type of university? In a word, research.

The emphasis on research above all other aspects of faculty work is the defining feature of doctoral universities. Doctoral universities try to attract and retain the best researchers in a particular field—being too heavy of a researcher is simply not a category that exists at doctoral universities. Consequently, the reward system for faculty is based on research productivity (Serow, 2000). Individual psychology departments have different definitions of research productivity, but according to one study, the average rate of publication in faculty's first five years at doctoral universities was two to three journal articles per year (Joy, 2006). Not all publications are created equal, however, because doctoral departments have weighting and ranking systems for how valuable specific publications are when evaluating faculty performance (H. L. Miller, Flores, & Tait, 2014). It is not just publish or perish; it is publish correctly or perish.

A corollary to being a productive researcher in most areas of psychology is obtaining grants. Nobody wants to pay participants or buy fancy eye-tracking hardware with their own money, and neither do universities. Applying for and receiving grants from external agencies is the solution. Receiving a large grant is a sign of research acumen for faculty members, and university administrators hold external grants in high regard because grants include funds that go directly to the university to offset institutional expenses. Thus, at doctoral institutions, securing external grants to fund research influences professors' chances for tenure and promotion (Serow, 2000).

The emphasis on research does not mean that teaching is irrelevant at doctoral universities or that the teaching is poor. However, the teaching load of individual faculty is typically very small, one or two courses a semester. Research grants can even be used to "buy out" of teaching responsibilities by securing funds to pay for replacement instructors. In terms of the quality of teaching, there are stellar teachers at doctoral universities, but expectations are not high—being adequate is adequate (Serow, 2000; Sternberg, 2017). Teaching garners attention when it is incompetent, not when it is great.

If you truly love the doctoral-university setting but want to emphasize teaching rather than research in your career, doctoral universities have positions that match those interests. Non–tenure-track instructors on short-term contracts do much of the undergraduate teaching at doctoral universities. Also, doctoral universities are increasingly adding positions that focus mostly or exclusively on instruction but offer some version of a continuing contract.

One of the unique aspects of work at a doctoral university is mentoring the next generation of psychologists. Teaching may focus extensively or exclusively on graduate courses, and advising focuses on graduate students who serve in the role of professional apprentices. When working with graduate students, doctoral faculty guide research projects, teach specialized scientific techniques, assist in manuscript revision, and generally bestow the unwritten rules of the profession. If the idea of teaching and mentoring a set of hand-selected, exceptionally talented and motivated students sounds like a dream come true to you, doctoral universities are your best chance to make it a reality.

Service is the final and least emphasized aspect of faculty work at doctoral universities, but there are some unique service opportunities that simply do not exist at colleges without extensive graduate programs. For example, doctoral universities typically have graduate admissions committees, graduate training directors, and undergraduate curriculum directors (Sternberg, 2017). There are some unique ways that doctoral university faculty provide service to the broader profession as well. The editorial boards of basic science journals, reviewers of cutting-edge grants, and top officers of professional organizations are virtually all made up of faculty from doctoral universities.

MASTER'S UNIVERSITIES

Master's universities, often referred to as regional or comprehensive universities, are easy to overlook because, possessing neither the research power of doctoral universities nor the singular focus on undergraduate education of baccalaureate or community colleges, they are the middle child of higher education (Henderson, 2011; Wright et al., 2004). Nonetheless, with almost 750 institutions enrolling about 4.5 million students, master's universities have a large footprint in terms of areas of the country represented and students served (Carnegie Classification of Institutions of Higher Education, 2016). Many master's universities' original mission was to educate undergraduates, but a desire to look more like doctoral universities and increase profits led to expansions into graduate education and research. Thus, part of the master's university mission is firmly rooted in undergraduate education, which is likely to be valued as high or higher than research, and part of the mission resides in the graduate training, which is associated with higher research expectations.

Requirements for faculty work at master's universities reflect their dual mission and give equal weight to teaching and scholarship. Achieving tenure requires publications (Sikorski & Bruce, 2014; Vazin, 2014; Woody & Alcorn, 2014), but faculty prioritize teaching first and do not publish at the furious rate of their colleagues at doctoral universities (Henderson, 2011; Youn & Price, 2009). Early-career psychology faculty at master's universities average about one publication a year (Joy, 2006). In addition, the combined mission of master's universities offers an environment that is particularly well suited to psychologists interested in merging their scholarship and their teaching.

The integrated nature of teaching and scholarship at master's universities can be seen in contributions to basic science journals versus pedagogical journals (Henderson & Buchanan, 2007). Faculty from master's universities make up only 4% of the authors of articles published in basic science journals and 0% of their editorial boards. In contrast, they make up 37% of the authors in pedagogical journals and 39% of the editorial boards. The mingling of scholarship and teaching can also be seen in the emphasis placed on providing research opportunities for undergraduates (Buddie, 2014; Critchfield & Jordan, 2014; R. L. Miller, 2014; Sikorski & Bruce, 2014; Vazin, 2014; Woody & Alcorn, 2014). In fact, for some departments, programmatic research and prolific publication are secondary to having ongoing projects that foster student involvement.

Although faculty at master's universities must maintain a research program, teaching is their primary responsibility. A load of three courses each semester is typical, but that may include multiple sections of the same class and, perhaps, release time for new faculty attempting to start a program of research (Critchfield & Jordan, 2014; R. L. Miller, 2014; Sikorski & Bruce, 2014; Woody & Alcorn, 2014). Not only are expectations for teaching quantity different at master's universities, so are expectations for teaching quality. Unlike doctoral universities, the promotion, tenure, and reward structures of master's universities reflect an equal or larger emphasis on teaching than research.

Service is an essential part of faculty life at master's universities, but it comes in a distant third in terms of importance. By some estimates, service counts half as much as scholarship and teaching, roughly 20% of workload (Critchfield & Jordan, 2014; Woody & Alcorn, 2014). Opportunities for service are much the same as at doctoral universities, but the increased emphasis on undergraduate education translates into more opportunities for work with undergraduates to count toward service. For example, undergraduate advising is more likely to be part of the workload at master's universities than at doctoral universities, and this can require contact with a substantial number of students each semester (Vazin, 2014). Graduate students, although fewer in number than undergraduates, need advising and mentorship of a more individualized nature. In other words, service, like teaching and research, will reflect the combined mission of master's universities.

BACCALAUREATE COLLEGES

If doctoral universities represent one popular conceptualization of higher education, baccalaureate colleges are their counterstereotype. Baccalaureate colleges are the institutions that come to mind when people say they went to a "private college" or a "liberal arts college." Although the number of institutions focused on 4-year degrees is enormous, almost 2,000 nationwide, they tend to be small and enroll fewer total students than any other type of institution (Carnegie Classification of Institutions of Higher Education, 2016). Baccalaureate colleges require balance in faculty roles, but there is no ambiguity in the prioritization of teaching over other responsibilities (Brakke, 2014; Milem, Berger, & Dey, 2000; National Center for Educational Statistics, 1997; Wright et al., 2004). Teaching typically represents 60% or more of the workload at baccalaureate colleges. As such, teaching is the primary category by which faculty are evaluated for tenure and promotion. At some elite colleges, the high standards for teaching are combined with expectations for scholarship that match those at doctoral universities, but the emphasis on teaching remains—research productivity must coincide with, not replace, excellence in undergraduate instruction.

The size and distinct missions of baccalaureate colleges affect professors' teaching responsibilities. Faculty are hired for their teaching at most baccalaureate colleges, not for expertise in some ultraspecialized area of research, and this means that faculty must be ready to teach broadly within their general area (Dunn & Zaremba, 1997). In addition, baccalaureate colleges tend to have general education programs with unique, oftentimes mission-specific, course offerings designed for all students, not just psychology majors (Troisi, Christopher, & Batsell, 2014). At baccalaureates, faculty members are dedicated to education at the college level, not just the departmental level.

The nature of work with students is also unique at baccalaureate colleges. Baccalaureate faculty are encouraged, if not expected, to take advantage of small class sizes by giving students individualized mentorship, teaching liberal arts skills, having exams that require writing, and, in general, assigning challenging work (Ault, 2014). A corollary to small classes and higher expectations is that students require and demand more personal attention from their teachers. Academic advising is particularly heavy for faculty at baccalaureate colleges (NACADA: The Global Community for Academic Advising, n.d.). Nonetheless, the good news is baccalaureate faculty members typically see interaction with students as one of the most positive aspects of their job (Marston & Brunetti, 2009).

Between all the teaching, grading, and mentorship, faculty at baccalaureate colleges must also find the time for scholarship. Generalizations about research at baccalaureate colleges are difficult to make because expectations vary so widely based on mission and resources (Brakke, 2014; McElroy & Prentice-Dunn, 2005). Early-career psychology faculty at elite baccalaureate colleges publish about twice a year, and the rate of publication is about half that at less-prestigious colleges (Joy, 2006). Beyond sheer rate of publication, research is especially valued if it affords meaningful opportunities for student involvement (Ault, 2014; Brakke, 2014; Dunn & Zaremba, 1997; R. L. Miller, 2014; Troisi et al., 2014). For faculty at baccalaureate colleges, research is a high-impact teaching practice.

Service is also a bigger part of faculty life at baccalaureate colleges than at master's or doctoral universities. Going along with their undergraduate-focused missions, faculty are expected to have open-door policies and to generally be available for formal and informal interactions with students (Ault, 2014; Dunn & Zaremba, 1997). In addition to students' need for attention, the institutions themselves can be demanding. Baccalaureate colleges have small faculty bodies but a lot of administrative work that needs to be done to keep departments running smoothly, curricula updated, accreditation agencies satiated, and so on. Furthermore, there is often a "college-first" mentality that encourages faculty to prioritize the college's needs over dedication to career or profession (Wright et al., 2004). As such, professors who have difficulty saying no or setting work–life boundaries may find themselves spending every waking moment recruiting students, serving on committees, supporting student extracurricular activities, and generally exhibiting a rah-rah spirit at every campus event; such work is meaningful but exhausting.

COMMUNITY COLLEGES

Community colleges are the invisible gorillas of higher education—huge but often overlooked. Of all undergraduate students, 45% attend community colleges, and this represents about 7 million students spread across more than 1,000 institutions (American Association of Community Colleges, 2016; Carnegie Classification of Institutions of Higher Education, 2016). Within psychology, more introductory psychology courses are taught at community colleges than anywhere else, and the number of associate's degrees awarded in psychology increased 352% in the first decade of the 2000s, which was the largest increase of any discipline (American Psychological Association, n.d.-a). Given their abundant campuses, vast student body, and national trends toward tuition-free enrollment (Juszkiewicz, 2016), community colleges are a shockingly overlooked career option for people seeking to be psychology professors.

More than the other three college types, community colleges have a unifying mission that cuts across individual institutions. The most distinctive and defining feature of the community college mission is their open-enrollment policies, and, yes, that means anyone can sign up to take courses (Provasnik & Planty, 2008). Educational goals at community colleges can include vocational training, earning an associate's degree, or transfer to a college with a 4-year program (Provasnik & Planty, 2008; Twombly & Townsend, 2008). By definition then, the mission of community colleges emphasizes lower level courses for students who are early in their programs of study. As the name implies, community colleges are structured around their local communities, both in terms of how they are funded and who they serve (Provasnik & Planty, 2008). Thus, community colleges are distributed throughout the United States and tend to draw both their students and faculty from local communities. Finally, the mission of community colleges is exclusively focused on undergraduate education, so faculty members are teachers first and foremost.

The unique mission of community colleges affects faculty work and their requisite qualifications. As much as 70% of faculty time is spent on teaching (Milem et al., 2000; National Center for Educational Statistics, 1997), and with five courses a semester being typical, teaching loads are higher than at any other type of institution (Center for Community College Student Engagement, 2016; Twombly & Townsend, 2008). The absence of scholarship from the community college mission translates into reduced value on faculty having doctorates. After all, the purpose of the doctorate of philosophy degree (PhD) is to train scientists who can produce original contributions to the research literature, and that is not a requirement of being a good teacher. A master's degree and 18 credit hours of graduate study in the to-be-instructed field are the standard qualifications for hiring (Twombly, 2005). Among all faculty members at community colleges, only 21% have doctorates (Center for Community College Student Engagement, 2016). Within psychology, the number is higher at 41%, but teaching with a master's degree remains standard (American Psychological Association, n.d.-a). Nonetheless, if competition is stiff, and if two equally good teachers are up for the same position, the edge will likely go to the candidate with a doctorate over a master's degree (Ewing, 2014).

Service is also a part of being a faculty member at a community college. In general, the expectation is that professors serve on college committees, typically at least one, and teaching-focused service is especially valued (Ewing, 2014; Franz, Manbur, & Neufeld, 2014; Rudmann, 2014). As would be expected from the institutional priority on teaching, the vast majority of community college faculty spend only a few hours a week on scholarship (Center for Community College Student Engagement, 2016), and they do not publish or present research on a consistent basis (Braxton & Lyken-Segosebe, 2015; Twombly & Townsend, 2008). Research is simply not part of the community college mission (Fugate & Amey, 2000; Rudmann, 2014). Conducting research is certainly a respected and valued activity, but it is not factored into the standard workload; it is an extra activity that community college faculty can engage in if so inspired.

VARIATIONS ON THEMES

As with any generalization, the four-types-of-college heuristic obscures some options in higher education employment. Here are some less common settings that might be of interest to people looking to for psychology positions.

Large Undergraduate-Only Colleges

Baccalaureate colleges are stereotypically small, but there are undergraduate- and teaching-focused institutions that are large. They may have some graduate programs, just not in psychology. Generally, these types of institutions are like master's universities without the requisite graduate programs.

Professional Schools

Some universities focus exclusively on professional training at the graduate level. Of course, many PsyD programs are housed in professional schools. However, there are other professions that require students to have practical knowledge of psychology. As such, psychologists can also become professors at universities exclusively dedicated to training professionals in areas as diverse as business, law, medicine, social work, optometry, or pharmacy.

Online Universities

The characteristics of online universities are just as varied as those of face-to-face universities. What makes them outliers is the fact that teaching occurs primarily or totally via course-management software. Course delivery is asynchronous and remote. Professors are largely unbound by time or location; they can work when and where they want as long as they are timely in administering instructional materials and responding to student needs. Thus, online universities offer more work flexibility than any other higher education setting.

CONCLUSION

What do you want to emphasize in your career? If research or teaching is your exclusive passion, then doctoral universities and community colleges are settings where professors focus most intensely on those single aspects of faculty work. If you desire balance, then master's universities and baccalaureate colleges offer a more equal mix of research and teaching. Of course, within each of these four categories, individual colleges provide variations capable of matching anyone's preferences. However, wanting a job as a professor at a specific type of institution and getting that job are two different things. Aspiring faculty need to build a CV with the research and teaching experiences needed to get hired. The next chapter outlines those experiences, as well as how to match them to each type of institution.

2

THE FUNDAMENTAL RESEARCH AND TEACHING EXPERIENCES NEEDED TO BE A PSYCHOLOGY PROFESSOR

Like many, or maybe even most, psychology professors, my career path was shaped by happenstance rather than strategic planning. When I started graduate school, I kept my professional goal to become a teacher hidden due to an unfounded paranoia that its discovery would lead to rejection by the research-focused faculty in my department. While furtively waiting for teaching opportunities, I published a few papers, largely because the department chose to fund me as a research assistant, but, once I started teaching, I kept up with research because I found it rewarding and fun. At the time, I was oblivious to how essential publications would be in my argument for why baccalaureate colleges should hire me as a professor. To my surprise, it was the combined experience of scholarship and teaching that eventually made me a competitive job candidate.

Aspiring professors need to pay their dues in graduate school by gaining a wide range of fundamental research and teaching experiences. There are several reasons why all graduate students, no matter their intended career path, should obtain basic experience in both areas. To begin, career goals can change. Formative experiences in research and teaching can lead graduate

http://dx.doi.org/10.1037/0000152-003
Becoming a Psychology Professor: Your Guide to Landing the Right Academic Job,
by G. A. Boysen

students who thought they were destined for a life in the lab or in the class-room in a new direction. In addition, graduate students need to be prepared for the fact that they may end up in jobs that do not perfectly match their career aspirations. The path to a dream job might start at a position with less-than-dreamy research or teaching requirements, and sometimes dreams and career realities never converge. Finally, in a competitive job market, a well-rounded curriculum vitae (CV) is needed to land any tenure-track position.

To help define what it means to have a well-rounded CV, this chapter outlines the research and teaching experiences needed to compete for faculty positions. Treat these research and teaching experiences not as a recipe for success but as a set of starting qualifications. To be truly successful in the job hunt, graduate students need to expand their CVs with experiences that appeal to their ideal type of institution. To help focus CV expansion efforts, this chapter also contains advice for matching research and teaching experiences to the four types of higher education institutions (for graduate school checklists related to research and teaching experiences, see the book's companion website: http://pubs.apa.org/books/supp/boysen/).

RESEARCH

Social psychologist Charles Lord's (2004) guide to graduate school in *The Compleat Academic* provided a stark assessment of the importance of research in finding an academic job. He argued that members of a search committee will spend just seconds on the first review of a candidate's CV, and having nothing listed under "Publications" means that the candidate is nothing to them—it is an automatic rejection. Difficult as it is to hear that a blank spot on a CV can obliterate all other professional accomplishments, everyone who wants to be a professor would be wise to eliminate scholarly black holes from their CVs before applying for jobs. Eliminating such holes requires graduate students to obtain research experiences and convert them into scholarly publications.

Research Experience

The Thesis and Dissertation
As a second-year graduate student, I proposed an overly elaborate master's thesis project focusing on a risky new area of study. My advisor considered the proposal and said, "Let's just write up your current project." With that sage advice, he saved me several semesters worth of work on a project that may or may not have succeeded, and he freed me up to start and finish

other projects. My advisor knew something that I did not: A thesis is but one project in a long career.

The master's thesis and doctoral dissertation are both necessary steps and valuable research experiences for aspiring faculty members. Excellent advice exists on how to successfully propose, conduct, and defend thesis and dissertation projects (Cone & Foster, 2006; Kuther, 2008), but the emphasis here is on using the project as a research experience that helps land a job. The most important advice is to plan a project that you can complete well before you start a full-time faculty position. Job applicants without a firm date for their dissertation defense seem like a risky bet when there are many candidates with degrees in hand.

The second most important advice is to plan a project that is publishable. Publications lead to job offers, so make publication a goal of every single research project in graduate school, especially the thesis and dissertation. With that in mind, write a dissertation that can be quickly and easily translated into a submission to a peer-reviewed journal. Ultimately, dissertations only matter in so far as they get you a degree and add to your list of publications (Kelsky, 2015). I have never had a conversation with any faculty member about his or her dissertation, and the only vestige of dissertations in professorial life is as a single line on a CV.

Research Assistantships

Assistantships typically consist of being assigned or selected to do research with a faculty member, often as a salaried employee on a grant-funded research project (Cope, Michalski, & Fowler, 2016; Kuther, 2008). It is a unique opportunity to learn that faculty member's area of study and earn credit as an author on presentations and publications stemming from the work. I had research assistantships early in my graduate career, and the work led directly to my first three publications and master's thesis. Faculty members get to choose students for assistantships, so making a good impression and being a productive researcher is key to continued funding and continued research opportunities (Kuther, 2008). If you are skillful in the work, your faculty advisor may eventually pass over responsibility for the conceptualization and design of studies over to you. At that point, you are officially being paid to do your own research, which is a true preview of professorship.

Managing a Lab and Research Assistants

If you are applying for positions that require research productivity, two standard interview questions you will face are "How will you set up a research lab here?" and "How will you incorporate students into your research?" Your answers to these questions will be more meaningful if you can draw on past experiences running a lab and working with research assistants. Leadership experience in the lab suggests that a graduate student has the potential to slip seamlessly into the managerial aspects of running a successful research program and, hopefully, administering large grants. One fundamental responsibility of professors is to provide opportunities for students to learn the science; ideally, that mentorship extends to opportunities for students to become coauthors on presentations and publications. Managing research assistants in the lab is the most direct way for graduate students to demonstrate their interest and skill in such mentorship.

Postdoctoral Research

Postdoctoral positions are not required to obtain a faculty position, but they are a way for doctoral graduates to gather additional research experience while employed under an experienced mentor. The positions are highly varied, but they typically emphasize research to the exclusion of teaching and service. So the logic is that postdoctoral study increases job competitiveness by increasing publications (McDermott & Braver, 2004; Schwebel & Karver, 2004). In addition, postdoctoral positions are a chance to expand research and grant-writing skills before having to implement them independently in a faculty position. Postdocs were once rare in psychology, but their prominence has increased, especially with the scarcity of full-time faculty positions (Pelham, n.d.; Schwebel & Karver, 2004). Despite increased prominence, less than a third of psychology doctorates do a postdoc, and they stay in the position for an average of only 2 years (Michalski, Kohout, Wicherski, & Hart, 2011; Wicherski, Michalski, & Kohout, 2009). Overall, postdocs are an increasingly important sign to search committees that job candidates will be able to immediately establish a productive program of research.

Presenting and Publishing Research

I spent an entire semester as a graduate student trying to validate a new, subtle measure of bias. Following a method outlined in a couple of articles from the previous decade, I designed a measure of linguistic bias showing that people tended to use abstract language when describing behaviors that are stereotypical of a group, or that was the goal anyway. In the end, months of planning, hundreds of surveys, and hours of analysis amounted to literally nothing. It just did not work. Although this failure taught me some valuable lessons about research, from a professional standpoint, the project and the semester spent on it represent a total blank spot in my career because they yielded no publishable material.

Gathering research experience is important, but so is turning that experience into peer-reviewed presentations and publications. Research that does not result in a product of some sort simply does not exist to the people who will eventually be evaluating your potential as a faculty member—the product, not the project, goes on the CV. With that in mind, what follows is an outline of the research products that graduate students should work toward.

Conference Presentations

Conference presentations are the training wheels of scientific productivity. They represent an opportunity for graduate students to share their initial scholarly ideas in a relatively low-stakes setting and begin to build a scientific reputation in their discipline. There are generally two tiers of presentations at psychology conferences: posters and oral presentations. Poster presentations have low prestige because of the low bar for acceptance, but they add a legitimate line to the CV with relatively little work or stress. Oral presentations have higher prestige because presenters either need to have research that is well known enough to be recruited for a panel or have to take it upon themselves to organize the panel. However, even a 10-minute slot on a panel can be a high-effort, high-stress affair. Of course, neither posters nor oral presentations are as prestigious or important as a peer-reviewed publication, which leads to a logical question: How many presentations should you do?

Academic lore suggests that one presentation a year is sufficient. The logic of not maximizing presentations is that the rewards of having multiple presentations a year do not outweigh the time and expense invested in presenting. Quantity of conference presentations is far less important to search committees than quantity of journal publications (Landrum & Clump, 2004), so time that would be spent on multiple presentations is better spent on nailing down a single publication. When you apply for a faculty position, search committee members may notice gap years when you did no presenting, but they will not be impressed by numerous presentations during a single year. In fact, having a significantly longer list of presentations than journal articles can give the impression of someone who cannot convert finished projects into publications. Basically, presentations are a way to demonstrate a consistent pattern of research activity, especially the early-career period when journal publications are less common.

Publications

The pressure to get publications has led to some rather nefarious activities (John, Loewenstein, & Prelec, 2012). Faking data, p hacking, stealing publication credit, selective reporting, and skipping institutional review board approval are just a few examples. Psychologists' willingness to put their professional reputation—and more important, the reputation of the science—in danger provides some perspective on just how important publications are to the careers of psychology professors.

Publications are fundamentally different from presentations because there is no theoretical limit to the value of adding more of them to a CV—more is always better. The number of publications a person has provides an objective sign of past productivity and future potential. Designing, executing, and writing a single study can take an entire year, and publications in top-tier journals typically require multiple studies; then it may be months until a submission is accepted or rejected—all of this for a single line on the CV (Kelsky, 2015; Lord, 2004). Given the time-intensive path to seeing even a single project through to publication, graduate students need to consider well before going on the job market how many publications they will need to be competitive for their ideal positions.

How many publications are needed? There is no research on the typical number of publications among applicants for faculty positions, but there are statistics for early-career psychologists (Byrnes, 2007; Joy, 2006). Within the first 5 years of employment, community colleges are the only setting in which most (65%) psychology faculty still have not published. In contrast, unpublished faculty make up less than 1% of professors at doctoral universities, 8% at elite baccalaureate colleges, 12% to 24% at master's universities, and 18% to 37% at less elite baccalaureate colleges. Basically, people starting off their career at every type of institution other than community colleges publish one article a year or more on average, and applicants for positions at these institutions should aim for at least that level of productivity.

Seeking Grants Large and Small

Here is an easy task to assess how seriously you should take getting grant experience in graduate school: Go to the webpage of a university where you would ideally work and evaluate the extensiveness of the office for sponsored programs, which is where administrators in charge of research funding and compliance reside. Is there no such office? Put grant writing way down on your professional development priority list. Does the office appear to be better funded than a small college? Move grant writing to second on your professional development priority list, right after publications.

Grant writing and management is like other aspects of faculty work; getting experience in graduate school makes you a better prepared professor and job candidate. The importance of securing external funding has grown as university budgets become tighter, especially at public institutions (Schwebel & Karver, 2004; Vazin, 2014). In some cases, external grants may be the only method faculty members have for funding graduate students and laboratories. Grant writing is a craft that requires practice and perseverance (Sternberg, 2004, 2017). Although graduate students are unlikely to be principle investigators on major grants, they can learn the craft by applying for modest grants that are not highly competitive. Internal university grants for research or travel are an ideal place to start, but small external grants are also within reach. A quick search of the webpages for professional organization produces information about dozens of grants ranging from hundreds of dollars to tens of thousands of dollars, and they fund everything from conference travel, to dissertations, to programmatic research. Large or small, funded or not funded, applying for grants is both a useful experience and a way to send a message about research potential.

Matching Research Experiences to Your Desired Job

Institution-specific differences need to be considered when deciding how much effort to devote to research. At community colleges, research is more or less irrelevant in the hiring process (Twombly, 2004, 2005). Not only are the colleges teaching-focused rather than research-focused, master's degrees, which do not require the extensive research training of doctoral degrees, are the standard qualification for employment. At the other end of the spectrum, publications are the most important factor in the evaluation of applicants at doctoral universities (Benson & Buskist, 2005). Postdoctoral study and experience with grant funding are also important (Landrum & Clump, 2004). It can be difficult to be hired at doctoral universities without postdoctoral experience, and it is impossible without an extensive record of publications in high-quality journals.

Baccalaureate colleges and master's universities emphasize more of a balance between teaching and research. At baccalaureate colleges, research is ranked behind teaching in hiring decisions (Benson & Buskist, 2005), but there is still an expectation that faculty be active scholars, especially at the elite institutions where research expectations are similar to doctoral universities. At master's universities, publications, research experience, and grants are emphasized, but search committees are likely to consider teaching experience as the most important factor (Benson & Buskist, 2005; Landrum & Clump, 2004). Because of the mixed mission of master's universities, productive scholars will be valued, but scholarship cannot obscure the absence of teaching interest and ability. A strong teacher with a strong publication record is the ideal candidate.

Even at institutions that heavily prioritize undergraduate teaching, research still needs to be considered (Adams, 2002). Search committees at smaller colleges with fewer resources will look at application materials with an eye for eliminating candidates with a repertoire of highly technical research methods that exceed their colleges' available facilities or budget. No, they will not be buying you an fMRI or building you a sleep lab. There may not even be a subject pool. Thus, it is valuable to have methodological flexibility that can be applied across many settings. Search committees will also pay attention to experiences with mentorship of student research. At baccalaureate colleges and master's universities, research should serve the mission of undergraduate education, so supervising research teams, mentoring students' projects, and getting students published are highly valued experiences.

TEACHING

Imagine going into surgery with a physician who was trained in the scientific foundations of medicine, who had published research in medical journals, but who had never completed a course on surgery or actually cut a person open. Such malpractice is impossible to conceive. In contrast, college professors are hired and given control over classes having literally no pedagogical training or experience. Most professors spend most of their time on teaching, and, in some positions, they spend virtually all of their time on teaching (American Association of University Professors, 2017; Morphew et al., 2016; National Center for Educational Statistics, 1997, 2003). As such, aspiring psychology professors should avoid pedagogical malpractice and make sure that they have the training and experience needed to take on the challenge and responsibility of teaching.

Pedagogical Training

Teaching is sort of like staging a play; the audience only sees an end product that gives them no sense of the work that goes on behind the scenes. Delivering a lecture or leading a discussion is the most visible part of teaching, but in-class time represents just a fraction of what teachers do. Courses on teaching provide future professors with an opportunity to learn about the backstage work that goes into the successful production and implementation of a college course. Teaching courses cover the basics of in-class teaching and learning techniques, but they also cover grading, preparation of course materials, ethics, how to handle difficult students, diversity, using technology, and many other things that novice teachers may have never realized fall into their job description (Buskist, Tears, Davis, & Rodrigue, 2002). In addition, almost all teaching courses include an opportunity to deliver a lesson and receive feedback.

Teacher preparation varies considerably across graduate programs (Beers, Hill, & Thompson, 2012), and, sadly, courses on teaching are not universal in doctoral programs. In fact, only about 65% of programs offer a credit-bearing course on teaching (Boysen, 2011; Buskist et al., 2002). If teaching courses are not available in psychology, there are other options. Other doctoral programs, such as those in higher education, may have teaching courses, or there may be college-wide courses offered through Preparing Future Faculty (http://www.preparing-faculty.org/) or general graduate studies programs. For example, some universities offer certificates in college teaching or in community college teaching. These are like graduate student minors that provide useful information about teaching, higher education, college students, and being a professor in general.

Classroom Experience

The most important teaching-related experience for aspiring professors is to get in front of a classroom and teach. In many programs, being a teaching assistant is the first instructional opportunity for graduate students, and there are several reasons to pursue such assistantships. To begin, teaching assistantships are a method for acquiring instructional skills and experience (Meyers & Prieto, 2000). In addition, the experience will help you determine how much you want to emphasize teaching in your career—many a die-hard researcher has shifted career focus after an experience in front of a classroom. Also, working under the supervision of an experienced teacher should lead to mentorship and a letter of recommendation that addresses teaching ability. Finally, doing well as a teaching assistant can open up opportunities for future teaching responsibilities, such as full responsibility for a course.

At some point, every professor steps into a classroom as the instructor of record with no one else dictating learning objectives, assignments, lesson plans, grading, or any of the other innumerable decisions that go into teaching a course. For both the professor and future search committees, no amount of work as a teaching assistant equals the experience of teaching one full course. Psychology departments have different policies and cultures when it comes to doling out teaching opportunities to needy graduate students. In the case that teaching a course will never be an option in your graduate program, look elsewhere. Teaching as an adjunct outside of your graduate institution is a viable option, especially with a master's degree. Regardless of where the course is taught, the experience will represent a serious shift in both your preparation to take on the responsibilities of being a professor and search committees' perception of your potential to successfully fill that role.

Matching Teaching Experiences to Your Desired Job

What teaching experiences do you need for what type of institution? Pedagogical training is not required to get a job anywhere because it is not available in all graduate programs, but baccalaureate college committees will appreciate it most, followed by teaching-focused master's universities. Committees at doctoral universities look less for such training because of their research focus. At community colleges, committees value teaching, but they do not require pedagogical training because they accept candidates with master's degrees and candidates who have had careers outside of academia.

The issue of how much teaching experience to obtain follows a similar pattern. Because teaching is central to their colleges' missions, no amount of teaching experience is too much for search committees at baccalaureate and community colleges. Entry-level positions at community colleges may even stipulate that qualified applicants must have been teaching for certain period of time (Jenkins, 2004a, 2014). People on the community-college job track need to start teaching well before they plan to apply for full-time jobs. In contrast, vast teaching experience may be off-putting to search committees at doctoral universities if it seems to have taken time away from publishing; however, if you are a highly productive scholar, extensive teaching experience is a bonus. Regardless of college type, being a teaching assistant for any number of courses will never count the same as teaching just one full course. Everyone should independently teach at least one full course before going on the job market.

Teaching experiences that match your desired institution will have the most value when applying for jobs. Teaching graduate courses will be directly relevant at doctoral and master's universities but will count for little at baccalaureate and community colleges other than general experience. Similarly, community colleges need teachers for lower level courses—especially introductory psychology—so advanced seminars in your specialty area are not directly relevant. Size matters. Doctoral and master's universities tend to have larger class sizes, so demonstrating the ability to manage large-enrollment courses is an advantage. Baccalaureate colleges emphasize small class sizes, so experience with courses of 50 or fewer students is most relevant.

What about the makeup of classes? Community college students represent a diverse array of backgrounds and abilities, so being able to demonstrate that you can reach both the most and the least prepared students will serve you well. If you are truly dedicated to a community college career, then pick up some courses as an adjunct at a local community college (Jenkins, 2004a). Being an adjunct carries no stigma at community colleges, and they will hire talented adjuncts for full-time positions. On the other end of the spectrum, elite colleges and universities (baccalaureates are especially guilty of this) may want evidence that you can offer courses rigorous enough to challenge their students, so gather experience with honors courses or specialized seminars if possible.

Finally, what methods should you have in your teaching toolbox? Search committees at every type of institution will appreciate a teacher who has expertly taught classes using a variety of methods, so mastery of many pedagogical skills is never a detriment. However, the extent to which you need to develop these skills does vary by institution. At doctoral and master's universities with large classes, having a solid record of lecture with some active learning to spice things up will be sufficient. At the smaller baccalaureate and community colleges, you need to provide evidence that you can meaningfully engage students in classes small enough for you to learn everyone's name. The same dynamic holds true for teaching liberal arts skills such as writing, speaking, and critical thinking. Here is a no-brainer: Search committees at baccalaureate colleges, sometimes referred to as liberal arts colleges, will especially be looking for teachers with pedagogical strategies for getting students to communicate effectively and think critically.

CONCLUSION

In writing this book, I talked with psychology professors from all types of institutions, and, no matter their background or current position, two themes emerged. First, they wished that they would have been able to learn more in grad school about what it means to be a professor and how to become one intentionally. Second, they loved their work. It is up to you to intentionally gather the experiences needed to be your ideal type of professor—teaching-focused, research-focused, or teaching- and research-focused—and it is also up to you to communicate those experiences to your future colleagues during the hiring process. Then, once you are a professor, you can continue the love affair with psychology that drew you to the field in the first place.

3 PROFESSIONAL SERVICE, ENGAGEMENT, AND CONNECTIONS

When I was in graduate school, one of my mentors involved me in the process of hiring a new faculty member. I learned a lot from the experience, but what stands out most was my mentor's advice that hiring a new faculty member is as important as picking a spouse. After all, you could be spending the rest of your working life with the new hire, and, if the person gets tenure, there is no such thing as an "academic divorce" should things go sour. My advisor's view of academic hires as being like adding a family member is not unique, and experts agree that hiring decisions can come down to who faculty would like to see in the office next door (Buddie, 2014; Keith & Zwokinski, 2014; Morgan & Landrum, 2012). Ultimately, faculty members want to hire someone with a reputation as an engaged and responsible professional.

Cultivation of a positive academic reputation is a career-long venture. Service is a core component of reputation building. Although service always falls behind research and teaching when evaluating job applicants' potential for success, productive scholars and teachers who also contribute to departmental and professional tasks have an edge over individuals who appear to

http://dx.doi.org/10.1037/0000152-004
Becoming a Psychology Professor: Your Guide to Landing the Right Academic Job,
by G. A. Boysen

shirk service duties. Reputations are also built by making connections within the professional community. Connections start with mentors in graduate school, but they increasingly include the maintenance of online presence as well. The academic world is exceedingly small. As such, aspiring professors must be unfailingly professional so that their careers are helped, rather than hurt, when their reputations precede them to potential colleagues (for graduate school checklists related to service and making connections, see this book's companion website: http://pubs.apa.org/books/supp/boysen/).

PROFESSIONAL SERVICE AND ENGAGEMENT

Service to Department and College

As an undergraduate, I remember being befuddled as I was sitting in the department lounge listening to my advisor talk with another professor about the goings on in some mysterious entity he was part of called the "Faculty Senate." And here all I thought he did was teach class, read books, and drink tea. To those outside of the faculty ranks, it may not be obvious just how much background work needs to be done to keep a college up and running. In fact, faculty participation in shared governance of the university is a fundamental principle in American higher education, and this requires their involvement in university-wide planning, policy making, budgeting, and hiring (American Association of University Professors, n.d.). Most people who apply for faculty jobs have some experience with service to their department or college (Sheehan & Haselhorst, 1999), and, although the weight of such experience always falls behind scholarship and teaching, it still contributes to the overall picture of a job candidate as being professionally productive and responsible.

Opportunities for graduate students to become involved with service are limited compared with full-time faculty, but there are some ways to contribute to departmental or college tasks (Morgan & Landrum, 2012; Sternberg, 2017). Graduate students can serve on admissions committees, curriculum committees, or student-body associations. Some of the same committees and associations will have appointed or elected roles for graduate students, and these leadership positions are a form of service. Graduate students can also serve as organizers by putting together professional workshops and seminars for topics of interest to them professionally. In addition, they may help the department prepare when guest speakers come to campus, plan academic events such as conferences, or organize receptions and meals when prospective students interview on campus.

There is one type of departmental service that graduate students should pursue at all costs: being on faculty search committees. Much can be learned from observing the faculty hiring process (Vick, Furlong, & Lurie, 2016; Wells, Schofield, Clerkin, & Sheets, 2013). The process itself, which can seem like a black box from the perspective of applicants, will be less mysterious if you have already worked on the inside. In addition, depending on the level of participation allowed to students, you might gain early insight into the effectiveness of various application materials, job talks, and interview strategies. Seeing candidates' successes and failures will provide a model of what to do and not do when you are in their position. At the very least, you might get a few free meals.

Professional Engagement and Service to the Profession

Before exploring ways to serve the profession, it is worth considering what it is to have a profession. Being in a profession means that you are part of a guild of people who have similar training and who offer similar services. Professional organizations advocate for the interests of their members, and joining these organizations is a way to demonstrate professional engagement. Although professional engagement is not a requirement to find a job, it is seen as a positive quality. Professional organizations abound in psychology. The American Psychological Association (APA) has 56 subdivisions organized by psychology topic, there are professional organizations based on U.S. regions, and each major area of psychology has its own, even more specialized, associations.

Professional organizations charge dues for membership, so how does the investment of joining professional organizations pay off? Larger organizations will have annual conferences that are essential opportunities to present research and stay up-to-date on the latest trends, and attendance is typically exclusive to or much cheaper for members. Professional organizations are also a way to connect with people in the field. Particularly in the case of more specialized organizations such as the Society of the Teaching of Psychology and the Psychonomic Society, there is no other place to find people more similarly aligned to your interests and goals. Finally, one major form of service is to help run professional organizations, and that work is for members only.

Even for graduate students, there are extensive opportunities for professional service. The major professional organizations each have specialized groups for graduate students. Graduate students joining the Association for Psychological Science (APS) automatically become a member of the Student

Caucus, and this allows them to become their campus representative or run for election to the national board. There are even more extensive opportunities through the APA. The American Psychological Association of Graduate Students (APAGS) provides opportunities to serve as officers, subcommittee members, and campus representatives, as well as ambassadors at the annual convention. APAGS even has representatives on APA committees going all the way up the board of directors, and it is difficult to imagine graduate students having access to a higher position of power in the profession.

Opportunities to serve psychology also exist outside of the professional organizations. Peer reviewing journal articles is often graduate students' first form of professional service (Kuther, 2008; Morgan & Landrum, 2012; Sternberg, 2017). Graduate students can also seek out reviewing opportunities for grants, awards, and conference programs. Mentors may help you find reviewing opportunities in your discipline, but there is nothing wrong with contacting editors and professional organizations to offer your services. That is exactly what I did at *Teaching of Psychology*, and the rewards have included great professional connections, several terms as a consulting editor, roles on journal working groups, and tons of interesting articles to read.

MATCHING PROFESSIONAL SERVICE AND ENGAGEMENT TO YOUR DESIRED JOB

Faculty value service at all types of institutions, but a simple rule to follow in pursuing service is to become involved in activities that best match what you want to emphasize in your career. Take the example of a graduate student in social psychology. If the plan is to become a professor at a doctoral or master's university, then the student should emphasize involvement in research-focused organizations like APS or the Society for Personality and Social Psychology. The student should also get as deep as possible into reviewing journal articles and grants. In terms of department or college service, it too should emphasize the promotion of scholarship. A key point, however, is that none of this service will count at all toward getting a job at a research-focused university unless you first have the requisite publication record.

If a social psychology graduate student is aiming for positions at community or baccalaureate colleges, the aforementioned organizations are still professionally relevant, especially considering their teaching-related programming, but the most relevant organization is the Society for the Teaching of Psychology. The Society even has a Graduate Student Teaching

Association specifically designed to promote the development of teachers (Society for the Teaching of Psychology, Graduate Student Teaching Association, 2017). If the goal is to teach at a community college, the student might join the APA's Psychology Teachers at Community Colleges network, or PT@CC (American Psychological Association, n.d.-a). In terms of department or college service, involvement in work related to teaching, curriculum, or assessment are most relevant. Once again, all the teaching-related service in the world will not make up for having little teaching experience when applying for jobs.

FACE-TO-FACE CONNECTIONS

Finding Mentors

Mentors have a significant impact on the professional lives of graduate students. Although it is easy to focus on mentors' roles as academic advisors or dissertation supervisors, they also serve career and psychosocial functions (Johnson, 2002; Johnson & Huwe, 2003). In terms of career functions, mentors ensure that their protégés receive challenging and developmentally appropriate opportunities that result in exposure to the field. They also coach protégés on the written and unwritten rules for success and protect them from professional dangers, both self-inflicted and external. In terms of psychosocial functions, mentors are role models for protégés, and they provide trusted support and counsel. Does this all sound like too much for one person to possibly accomplish? It is, and that is why graduate students often have multiple formal and informal mentors who play different roles and fulfill different needs.

The process of finding a mentor occurs both formally and informally. Graduate programs may assign mentors by placing each student under the supervision of a faculty advisor, or they may require students and faculty to match up based on open positions, funding, and shared interests (Johnson & Huwe, 2003; Kuther, 2008). Administrators in charge of running grad programs believe that these procedures lead nearly all students to find formal mentors (Dickinson & Johnson, 2000; Johnson, 2002), but less than half of graduate students perceive themselves as being mentored (Clark, Harden, & Johnson, 2000; Johnson, 2002). Thus, graduate students should be prepared to intentionally seek out a mentor if their program does not provide one.

Informal mentors can be just as important as formal ones. The search for informal mentors begins with departmental faculty. Get to know them by taking their classes, attending their research talks, and working with them on projects (Morgan & Landrum, 2012; Sternberg, 2017; Vick et al., 2016). One rewarding, but scary, way to seek out mentors is to make contact with faculty members from other institutions who are leaders in your field of study (Johnson & Huwe, 2003; Kelsky, 2015; Vick et al., 2016). A strategic email or introduction at a conference can do wonders for your career. To aid in these types of professional connections, many organizations, including APA and its divisions, have programs to connect graduate students with like-minded mentors. Finally, do not count out peers as valuable mentors (Johnson & Huwe, 2003; Kuther, 2008). Other students in your program may hold perspectives or information that is of value to your professional development.

Women and people from diverse backgrounds often find it rewarding to have mentors who share a similar background. Shared experiences can make mentorship more comfortable, and the mentor will have relevant insights about overcoming barriers to success (Johnson & Huwe, 2003). So, women and people from diverse backgrounds can benefit from having multiple mentors who all play specialized roles in their career development (APA, 2009, 2010). In recognition of the difficulty some students can have finding a mentor with the same background, the APA and other professional organizations have set up specialized mentorship programs for people with diverse backgrounds, and details can be found on their websites.

Departmental Collegiality

The challenges of being a professor tend to be of the good, intellectual variety, but, looking back on my career, the most stressful experiences were all caused by other professors' bad behavior. Terrible people can lurk in the dark corners of academia. As such, departments strive to avoid adding high-maintenance, high-drama faculty to their ranks (Boysen, Morton, & Nieves, in press). Applying for a job requires uniformly positive recommendation letters from several faculty members who know you well, and search committees may do back-channel reconnaissance by connecting with other people in your department who did not serve as a reference (Morgan & Landrum, 2012; Vick et al., 2016). Any whiff of uncollegial behavior can lead to immediate rejection of a job candidate.

To maintain a good reputation, graduate students should avoid all departmental drama, infighting, and politics, especially if any of this involves faculty (Kuther, 2008). They should also strive to be respectful, positive, and professional during classes, at meetings, at departmental parties, during colloquia, and across all other professional interactions with everyone from the department chair to the department secretary. Something as simple as a bout of in-class petulance, a biting question during a colloquium, or a drunken jest at a party could taint an otherwise glowing reputation for collegiality. It is a small world, so act like it.

ONLINE CONNECTIONS

In his book, *So You've Been Publicly Shamed*, journalist Jon Ronson (2016) shared the story of a woman who tweeted the message "Going to Africa. Hope I don't get AIDS. Just kidding. I'm white!" before getting on a flight to Cape Town. Although she intended the message to be a satirical joke for her 170 Twitter followers, by the time her plane landed, she was the target of worldwide derision on Twitter. And she had been fired. In the age of social media, a ruined life is just a few keystrokes away.

Cautionary tales aside, can a modern-day academic afford to be a Luddite when it comes to having an identifiable reputation online? Job candidates get Googled—it's just a fact. If you have a nefarious past with a long string of narrow escapes from felony convictions, the problem with your online reputation is obvious, but some argue that getting no hits with a candidate's name is also problematic (Kelsky, 2015). It is now considered abnormal to be a ghost online. Having a page or two of positive links pop up when searching your name online will not lead to a job offer, but making online connections is an increasingly important tool for connecting to colleagues and establishing a professional reputation.

Social Networking

Would B. F. Skinner have accepted your friend request? Wonder no more because there are dozens and dozens of B. F. Skinners on Facebook. My personal favorite is "B.f. Skinner" who describes himself as "self-employed," has a relationship status of "it's complicated," and has such luminary friends as Carl Jung, John Dewey, and Wilhelm Wundt. Social networking is not all silliness and lies, however, because, in addition to Facebook, there are Facebook-like websites for academics. Millions of academics and researchers use social networking websites such as Academia.edu and ResearchGate. To paraphrase *The Social Network*, people do not go to these sites to read about famous scientists. They can do that in textbooks and journals. No, they go to read about scientists that they know.

Academia.edu and ResearchGate are the major social networking sites for academics, and they have many of the same features. Starting a basic account is free and allows you to customize a profile page containing information about your research and professional background. Once you have a profile, the social networking can begin as you connect with and follow the activities of scholars in your field. The sites will suggest possible connections based on your interests, and they both have search functions through which you can look up people or topics and follow the chain of research connections. If you have publications to add, the websites will automatically create a list of them for you, and you have the option to upload data, papers, and other research materials so that they are available to other scientists. Arguably, the sites' true popularity, and questionable legality, stems from the ability to obtain published papers for free from other scientists, and one clear advantage of having your research on the social networking sites is that you and your work can be easily identified by other researchers and by potential employers.

Blogs and Twitter

If a psychologist's goal is to share an idea as quickly as possible, there may be no better outlet than blogs and Twitter. Ideas can be transferred from your mind to the world as fast as you can type. But will anyone care? It depends. For many years I have had a course blog where students post short entries that bust psychological myths. I did literally nothing to publicize the blog outside of my university until I sent the link out in a post to an email list for psychology teachers. After that posting, it received more visitors and page views in 2 days than it had in total for any previous year. Online posts can be useful to spread your ideas and to network with like-minded psychologists, but you have to bring the posts to the people rather than waiting to be discovered.

Experts have provided some recommendations for how to approach blogs and Twitter as professional tools. One thing to keep in mind is that these platforms are more useful for social networking than as a form of high-impact scholarly communication (Kelsky, 2015; Sternberg, 2017). Citations in journals are still the gold standard for quality in scholarship. In contrast, number of page views or Twitter followers is not going lead to a job offer or tenure. Nonetheless, high counts on these metrics, by definition, translate into more professional visibility.

Scholarly communication in psychology occurs almost entirely through journal articles, so there are no rules for online platforms such as blogs and Twitter (Vick et al., 2016). Although the absence of rules allows you to be creative in ways that are impossible with traditional professional publication outlets, you have to be more intentional in choosing what and how you post. Without editors and peer reviewers to point out bad ideas, there is a danger of making yourself look silly, or worse. For example, consumer-behavior researcher Brian Wansink self-destructed his academic career by making a blog post that seemed to suggest that his lab massaged significant results out of data by any means necessary (Bartlett, 2017). One sentence in one blog led to nightmarish levels of professional scrutiny and his eventual resignation. Online is immediate and forever. Be careful, and take it slow (Vick et al., 2016).

Websites

Making recommendations about professional websites seems quaint after discussion of modern social media, almost like going into detail on how to calculate analyses of variance most efficiently by hand. Nonetheless, websites can be an important part of a psychologists' online presence. It is common for academics to have personal or laboratory websites on which they share a professional profile, publications, research materials, teaching materials, and a CV. This is much the same as what gets posted on the profile pages of academic social media websites such as Academia.edu and ResearchGate. Nonetheless, the advantages of a website are that you have complete control over the design and visitors will have direct access to all of your materials without creating an account.

Websites do have downsides (Kelsky, 2015). One problem is the difficulty in keeping them updated. Having a gratuitously out-of-date website makes a worse impression than having no website at all. Websites also require you to pick a professional persona that you want to project, and that persona had better match the job you eventually want to obtain. For example, search committees at teaching-focused institutions will look with suspect upon a candidate whose application materials portray a passion for teaching but whose webpage focuses exclusively on scholarship. Finally, no matter how cute or special you believe your cats or your kids to be, their pictures belong on Facebook (Kelsky, 2015). Keep personal stuff off your professional website.

MATCHING PROFESSIONAL CONNECTIONS TO YOUR DESIRED JOB

The advice for matching connections to a desired job is simple—connect with people doing what you want to do. When seeking out mentors, formal and informal, try to find ones who align with your relative career emphasis on research and teaching. If your goal is to work at a doctoral or master's university, find mentors who can include you in research projects and connect you to potential collaborators at other universities. Although your primary academic advisor is most important in this regard, involvement with other faculty in your department only increases the chances of research success. Also, take advantage of mentorship programs in your most closely aligned professional organization; this is most important for people seeking doctoral university jobs because of the importance of networking and collaboration in research. People on the path to baccalaureate or community colleges may have to do more work finding mentors than their research-focused peers. To be frank, it can be difficult or impossible to find pedagogical mentorship in some doctoral programs, so do not hesitate to find informal mentors who can provide teaching-focused advice and guidance. These mentors can come from other departments—good teaching cuts across disciplines—or even different institutions.

Do you need a website, blog, ResearchGate profile, or anything else online to get a job? Currently, the answer is no. However, elite doctoral universities strive to be influential and to have a national, or even international, reputations. As such, they will be more impressed by job candidates who can show evidence of being influential online. That being said, search committees at those elite doctoral universities will be much more impressed by extra publications than by any number of online followers. The main way that an online presence can help your career is by connecting with people in your field. No matter your career goal, network socially with people doing the job you eventually want to have. Also, post things online that are professionally consistent with what you want eventually to emphasize in your career, be that research, teaching, or a combination of the two.

CONCLUSION

Think of the most successful psychology professors that you know. Do they hole up in their offices, only emerging from isolation to deliver brilliant manuscripts and lectures? No, I bet they are broadly connected and engaged. There simply is no way to become a professor without being engaged and making professional connections. Even applying for a position requires securing several people in the profession who will vouch for your potential. Certainly, engagement and connections can be left to fate, but the most successful psychologists are also masters at cultivating professional networks.

4

SEARCHING FOR AND SELECTING OPEN POSITIONS

Having gotten my bachelor's degree from a private baccalaureate college, when it came time to apply for jobs in graduate school, I naturally favored a return to a private baccalaureate college. So, I was surprised to find myself drawn to the State University of New York at Fredonia. Despite having "State University" in the name, all of the characteristics that led me to prioritize private baccalaureate colleges were there: small class sizes, emphasis on teaching undergraduates, and support for student–faculty research. Despite my baccalaureate preference, it seemed like a perfect fit. My intuition turned out to be correct because they hired me, and I had a productive time there as an early-career psychologist.

How could a school that I was automatically biased against become my first choice? Colleges have many characteristics, and the job search process requires you to determine which ones are most important. Perhaps you are looking for a job any place that will allow you to continue your specialized field of research. Maybe family commitments have you locked into a single city. Or your passion might be for working with first-generation college students in need of extra academic support. Specialty area, geography, and

http://dx.doi.org/10.1037/0000152-005
Becoming a Psychology Professor: Your Guide to Landing the Right Academic Job, by G. A. Boysen

college type are just some of the factors to consider when deciding what job advertisements to pursue. The purpose of this chapter is to outline the choices you need to make in searching for a position, the ways to find advertisements for open positions, and how to interpret those advertisements. By making the right choices and interpretations, you increase the chance of matching your professional goals and talents to the needs of a department.

WHEN TO START THE JOB-SEARCH PROCESS

Starting the job-search process requires you to set a timeline for going on the market. Advertisements for full-time positions emerge mostly during the fall. Advertisements for part-time and visiting positions tend to emerge in the spring or, in some cases, just moments before the start of the fall semester. So, should graduate students apply the year they are scheduled to graduate regardless of where they are in their professional development? Or is it best to wait until they have amassed a war chest full of publications and teaching experience?

Going on the job market is never a sure thing. You cannot know how many open positions there will be, the number of other job seekers, how many more publications might come through by delaying a year, the vicissitudes of search committees, or a million other variables that might affect your lot. Comparing these unknowns with the known expense of staying in graduate school, one strategy is to apply for jobs as early as possible because you can always try again later, only with a stronger record and more experience (Kelsky, 2015).

How do first-timers do on the job market? One study found that it was the first year on the market for 32% of hires and 47% of people who went unhired (Ng, 1997). In other words, time and experience increases your chances of getting hired, but a significant number of people are getting hired on their first try. In general, the straightforward answer is to apply only when you have a strong enough record to get a job (Vick, Furlong, & Lurie, 2016). Evaluating your strength is far from an exact science, however.

Once you decide to go on the market, there is a lot to get done. A job-search timeline can be found in the Appendix to this volume. You can think of the search process as officially starting the year before you apply for positions, and one of the most important steps in the process is determining how far and wide you will send out applications.

DETERMINING YOUR SEARCH PARAMETERS

One of the most basic questions about the search process is: "How widely should I apply for positions?" Opinions vary. Research shows that people seeking psychology jobs send out 10 to 15 applications on average, but the standard deviation is huge—some people send out one, and others send out dozens (Demaray, Carlson, & Hodgson, 2003; Follette & Klesges, 1988; Gore, Murdock, & Haley, 1998). As illustrated by this wide range, there are multiple strategies for the hunt. One approach is to cast a wide net and apply for every position even remotely related to your specialty area—perhaps even some that are not remotely related. Alternatively, you can go for only the best shots and apply narrowly for positions that match your specific interests and qualifications.

Applying Broadly Versus Narrowly

Casting a wide net is intuitively appealing because applying for more positions seems like it should increase the chances of getting an interview—a wider net catches more fish. One way of thinking about sending out applications to many colleges is that because it is a buyer's market, having a narrow pool of job options is not in your interest (Iacono, 1981). If you have a rare piece of art that everyone wants, then you can be picky about how to sell it. In contrast, if you are trying to unload an old TV, then you should advertise far and wide to find a buyer because of the ample supply of similar merchandise. Sorry, but you are the old TV in this analogy, and the buyer's market makes it sound economic advice to advertise yourself far and wide.

Taking a broad approach requires you to apply for positions that are not a perfect fit, but some argue that this is worth the risk (Huang-Pollock & Mikami, 2007). The final pool of applicants for a position may include no one who is a perfect fit, leaving the door open for people with excellent qualifications but who do not exactly match the job requirements as advertised. Also, it can be difficult to judge fit from the outside. One analysis of the match between candidates' curriculum vitae (CVs) and the qualifications listed in job advertisements showed that the degree of match was identical for applications that led to interviews and those that did not (Horner, Pape, & O'Connor, 2001). Overall, why not let search committees eliminate you from the pool of candidates rather than eliminating yourself?

Perhaps you are now ready to spam every psychology department in the country with your application materials. Slow down and consider the merits of applying narrowly. From the perspective of the search committee, applications that do not fit the position are a waste of time (Darley & Zanna, 2004; Iacono, 1981). Search committees carefully choose the characteristics that they list in advertisements to fit the needs of the department (Brakke, 2014). They are not going to see your excellent but unrelated qualifications, fall in love, and ignore what they originally wanted. Casting a wide net also leads applicants to submit generic materials, and committees will spot and eliminate applicants whose materials are not tailored to a position (Boysen, Morton, & Nieves, in press; Brems, Lampman, & Johnson, 1995; Landrum & Clump, 2004).

Taking a narrow approach is also backed by research showing that fit determines who gets interviewed and hired. Search committee chairs indicate that fit with department needs is the most important factor in evaluating job candidates (Landrum & Clump, 2004; Ng, 1997). In addition, examination of the characteristics of people who are hired for positions illustrates that they typically meet all of the requirements listed in the job advertisement: This bears repeating, perfect matches get hired (Follette & Klesges, 1988; Gore et al., 1998). Having excellent qualifications only matters if those qualifications fit a department's needs.

Also consider your own needs. Do not apply for jobs that you would not accept (Darley & Zanna, 2004). There is no reason to put up a false front about fit because, in the end, neither you nor your new department will be happy with a bad fit (Anziano & Burke, 2014; Boyd, Caraway, & Flores Niemann, 2017). Also, leaving a faculty position can be awkward and painful on both sides; avoiding an academic breakup is in everyone's best interest.

Overall, my advice is to be selective. Only apply for positions, be it five or 50, that are a good fit and that excite you. The search committee will sense the excitement in your materials, and you will be excited about getting and keeping the job. If selectivity is required, how do you narrow down the large pool of open positions?

Narrowing by Specialty Area

Answer quickly. What type of psychologist are you? Your reply to that question sets the parameter for selection of a specialty area. Although I am tempted to end this section with those simple instructions, some explaining may help you avoid the mistake I made as a grad student in applying for jobs in three specialty areas. I look back on that choice with roughly the same level of chagrin as my teenage choice to leave the house sporting a mullet and a fanny pack. A candidate's specialty area represents the most strict and obvious criterion for fit with a position. Degree type and specialty area are the first things that search committee members will look for on a CV, and if the specialty area does not match the requirements of the position, they may be the last things looked at as well.

Search for jobs that match your degree, research specialty, and teaching expertise. If you are in a social psychologist, search for social psych jobs. If you are a clinical psychologist, search for positions open to applicants with a clinical/counseling background. What if you are one of those combination psychologists? The cognitive neuroscience, clinical health, cognitive developmental, and other interdisciplinary psychologists among us may plausibly search for positions of three different types, but even their records will provide them with a stronger case for one area or another based on their teaching and research experiences.

Narrowing by Geography

When advising undergraduates about selecting a graduate school, I start by asking what type of program they are interested in, but my second question is whether they are applying nationally or regionally. Job selection works the same way. The number of jobs available increases with the size of the geographic region being searched. Thus, setting search parameters to include as many regions as possible is one way to maximize opportunities. Experts have long advised against eliminating perfectly good jobs on the basis of location alone (Darley & Zanna, 2004). Does applying for a job in a place you have never been to, or perhaps even heard of, sound scary? It can be, and you have to decide on your acceptable balance of career opportunity and lifestyle security.

A national search provides the most chances for success, but it does pose some unique challenges. Fair-minded as academics claim to be, they have stereotypes about the desirability of living in certain locations. If you work 15 minutes from the beach or in a major metropolitan area and are applying for positions at landlocked, rural colleges, make it clear why such a move is the best thing for your career (no offense, I work at a landlocked rural college). A related issue is that community colleges tend to hire locally, and they may give less consideration to applications from far-flung areas unless candidates articulate clear reasons for their interest. Plus, community colleges will not pay for your travel if you are asked to interview on campus.

A national search does not fit everyone's lifestyle, and searches that focus on one region, despite netting fewer job openings, can still pay off. There are many ways to define a region. Some job-listing websites, a topic discussed at length later, will organize advertisements by geographic region of the

United States, such as the Northeast and Southwest, but it is most common to see advertisements organized by state. An easy way to set a regional parameter is to draw a circle on the map and search for open positions in any state that falls within that circle.

Some regional searches must be even more granular. Do you need to narrow your search to a specific city? Some websites allow job searches by metro region or zip code. This type of ultraregional search severely limits the number of available job openings. If you are locked into a small region and want to get a foot in the door irrespective of position availability, some experts suggest that you contact local departments, provide them with your credentials, and ask them to keep you in mind for future openings (Darley & Zanna, 2004; Vick et al., 2016). The recommendation to make unsolicited job contacts comes with two caveats. First, it is unlikely to yield a tenure-track position. Second, you can build a bad reputation at a college by seeming desperate to find a position there at any cost, especially if you repeatedly apply for positions that are not a good fit. Try to focus exclusively on open positions that are a good fit.

Narrowing by Type of College

Once you have a list of open positions in a specific region that match your specialty area, the next step is to see if they are at your preferred type of institution. The broadest, and most useful, heuristic is to filter positions into the four categories used throughout this book: doctoral universities, master's universities, baccalaureate colleges, and community colleges. Both the name of an institution and details in the advertisement will provide strong clues as to category, but a little research on the school's website, college ranking websites, or the Carnegie Classification website will provide all the information that you need at this point in the search. Although the heuristic is useful, keep in mind that the variations within the categories can be as great as those between the categories and that institutions often employ different types of professors. Always give priority to job characteristics over institution type (for a self-assessment based on preferences for college characteristics, see the book's companion website: http://pubs.apa.org/books/supp/boysen/).

FINDING JOB ADVERTISEMENTS

Once you have a firm idea of what you are looking for in a position, it is time to find job advertisements. In the not-so-distant past, the emergence of fall colors coincided a thickening of the *APA Monitor on Psychology* as the classified section expanded with dozens of new job postings. I remember being a graduate student on the job hunt and ripping my way to the back of the *Monitor* every month in hope of finding jobs in states close enough to home so as not to give my fiancée a panic attack. Traditional print ads still exist, but online advertisements are now standard. Online job advertisements are in everyone's best interests. They are freely accessible, frequently updated, easily monitored, and searchable using automatic and customizable tools.

Announcements for psychology positions come out in both psychology-specific sources and sources that cover all of higher education. Table 4.1 summarizes the main sources for information about job openings and each source's basic features. With numerous options available for finding job advertisements, what should your strategy be for using these resources? Diversify and automate. Using just one source for all your information might lead to you miss jobs, so you should diversify your search across several websites. With the ease of setting up automatic searches, there is no reason not to do so on every major job website—sure, there will be some overlap in the information that you receive, but it is better to have false alarms than misses in the job search process. As an additional source of unofficial information and rumor, you can skim the academic job wiki, but do not rely on this as your only source of information.

Institutions with commitments to hiring diverse faculty often publish their job advertisements in outlets that are of special interests to racial and ethnic groups. For example, some institutions place advertisements in publications such as *Diverse: Issues in Higher Education, Hispanic Outline on Education Magazine,* and *Tribal College Journal of Higher Education.* Another outlet is the online job boards of organizations of diverse psychologists, such as the Asian American Psychology Association, the Association of Black Psychologists, and the Society of Indian Psychologists. Although the jobs will be listed in other sources as well, their placement in diversity-specific outlets is an intentional sign of welcome to diverse applicants.

INTERPRETING THE WRITTEN AND UNWRITTEN MESSAGES IN JOB ADVERTISEMENTS

Once you know what type of position you want and how to find open positions, you are left with the substantial task of interpreting the arcane language of job advertisements. Consider the following hypothetical example:

> The Department of Psychological Sciences at Necker University announces a 9-month, open-rank, open-specialty, tenure-track position. We will consider

TABLE 4.1. Sources of Job Advertisements

Source	Description	Website search parameters	Website personalization
Psychology specific			
American Psychological Association (APA)	APA provides the most extensive listing of psychology-specific jobs. Listings are available on the website (http://www.psyccareers.com), and some are published in the APA *Monitor on Psychology*.	• Position type (title) • College type • State • Country	• Personal account • Personalized job alerts • Savable jobs • Savable searchers
Association for Psychological Science (APS)	APS emphasizes faculty and research jobs. Listings are available on the website (http://www.psychologicalscience.org/employment), and some are published in the *APS Observer*.	• Area of psychology • Full-/part-time • State	• General alert
Psychology Academic Job Search Wiki	Both employers and job seekers can add jobs to the wiki and update the status of the search (http://www.psychjobsearch.wikidot.com). Accuracy of information cannot be guaranteed.	• Area of psychology	• None
Higher education specific			
The Chronicle of Higher Education	*The Chronicle* is a higher education trade paper. Job listings span all types of higher education positions. Listings are available on the website (http://www.chroniclevitae.com), and some are posted in the printed paper.	• Field (social science) • State • College type • Full-/part-time • Distance from zip code	• Personal account • Personalized job alerts • Savable jobs • Savable searches

	Description	Search options	Features
HigherEdJobs	HigherEdJobs is a company specifically focused on employment. Job listings span all types of higher education positions. Listings are available on the website (http://www.highedjobs.com).	• Field (psychology) • Region of the United States • State • Metro region • Full-/part-time • College type	• Personal account • Personalized job alerts • Savable jobs • Savable searchers • Institution descriptions
Inside Higher Ed	*Inside Higher Ed* is an online news source about higher education. Job listings are available on the website (careers.insidehighered.com).	• Field (psychology & behavioral science) • Region of United States • State or city location • Distance from location • Full-/part-time • College type	• Personal account • Personalized job alerts • Savable jobs • Savable searchers • Institution descriptions
Higher Education Retention Consortium (HERC)	HERC consists of regional consortiums of organizations seeking to fill all types of higher education positions. Regional HERCs allow job seekers to find and apply for jobs using the website (hercjobs.org).	• Field (social/behavioral sciences) • Full-/part-time • State • Dual-career positions	• Personal account • Personalized job alerts • Savable jobs • Savable searchers • Apply for jobs

accomplished scholar–educators from across the subfields of psychology, but we are especially interested in individuals who can contribute to our new neuroscience curriculum. Candidates should be able to establish a program of independent research resulting in publications in scholarly journals. The teaching load is 3–3 with opportunities for release to reflect ongoing supervision of student research. Experience teaching statistics and methods is preferred. Doctoral candidates are eligible pending completion of their dissertation.

Confused? The Necker faculty are sending some mixed messages here— open position but neuroscience preferred, research but also teaching, 3–3 load but release possible, candidates should be accomplished but they can be finishing up their dissertation? This type of Rorschach-style advertisement is commonplace, but there are some interpretive rules you can follow to prevent yourself from projecting the wrong characteristics onto the position.

Job Responsibilities

The most important differentiation to make between job advertisements is that between teaching-focused positions and research-focused positions. Here are the first two big signals. One, if teaching or research is not mentioned in the ad, then the institution does not emphasize it. Two, if teaching or research is mentioned first, then the institution emphasizes it more. Next, there are some telling phrases that point toward a teaching or research emphasis. Advertisements for teaching-focused institutions include phrases such as the following:

- "excellence in undergraduate instruction,"
- "dedication to the liberal arts,"
- "contribute to a unique general education,"
- "provide meaningful research experiences for undergraduates,"
- "commitment to undergraduate education,"
- "student-centered," and
- "student-engagement."

In contrast, research-focused institutions will signal the importance of scholarship through phrases such as the following:

- "establish an independent program of research,"
- "publish in top journals,"
- "secure external funding,"
- "build a national reputation," and
- "conduct state-of-the-art work."

If an advertisement contains both types of signal words, the institution is, or wants to be, one of the truly elite colleges that requires faculty to be both accomplished scholars and talented undergraduate instructors.

Course load is another strong indicator of teaching focus. *Load* is described as the number of courses or credits taught each semester. A 3–3 load indicates a requirement to teach six courses a school year. There is some ambiguity here because courses may be three or four credits, and the difference between teaching a 3–3 load of 18 versus 24 credits is substantial. Not all advertisements will specify the number of courses that faculty members teach, but the numbers, when included, are an unmistakable signal.

Any load at or above four courses or 12 credits a semester is a straightforward indication of strong teaching emphasis—publication may not even be required for tenure. Loads of 2–2 and below are standard at doctoral universities. As you might expect, 3–3 loads split the difference and are likely to occur at places like master's universities where teaching is valued but there are firm expectations for research productivity. A related sign indicative of high research expectations is when advertisements mention release time from teaching to conduct research. Teaching is not replaceable with research at teaching-focused institutions.

Qualifications

More interpretive analysis is needed to discern what qualifications are needed to be a serious contender for a position. To begin, if the advertisement says that you need a doctorate, then you need one. But do you need one before you apply? If an advertisement says that a certain degree is required and nothing else, then you are safe applying as a student finishing up the requirements for that degree. Some advertisements will stipulate "ABD considered" or "degree in hand before start date," and this means that graduate students will receive full consideration, but they are concerned about getting burned by hires who cannot finish up their degrees.

Job candidates are unlikely to apply for positions without a required degree, but applications flood in from people whose degree is in the wrong specialty area. If an area of specialty is mentioned in an advertisement, search committees will look for that specialty on applicants' CVs, in their coursework, and in their teaching and research experiences. Being vague or skirting the issue will not fool them. This is especially true for clinical and applied positions where licensure or certification is required; accreditation requirements may stipulate the exact credentials needed by faculty in such programs. That being said, there are varying perspectives on whether being license eligible matters for professors who exclusively teach undergraduates

(Matthews, 2000), and search committees from teaching-focused colleges may intentionally leave licensure or the ability to practice out of advertisements status because they prioritize teaching ability above all else. So, do not eliminate yourself from such positions just because you are not licensed.

Some advertisements come out without dictating a specialty area, and these "open specialty" advertisements are perplexing—there really is no preference? In some cases, yes, it really is open. In other cases, there are indications in the advertisement what type of psychologist the committee is, at least implicitly, hoping to hire. If a position is open but "preference will be given to candidates with a background in . . . ," this is a strong indication that it is not really open at all. Similarly, advertisements that say the position is open but "preference will be given to candidates who can teach cognitive psychology, perception, and biopsychology" or "preference will be given to people whose research can take advantage of the new Center for Child Development" clearly suggests that there is a preferred specialty area.

It is always necessary to take preferred teaching and research specialties seriously. Courses need to be covered, and committees will give preference to candidates who can provide that coverage. If an advertisement outlines three courses that applicants must be able to teach and you can only cover one of them, that is a poor fit. Sure, you can lie about your teaching interests—both to the committee and yourself—but do you really want to be stuck teaching courses outside of your interests and expertise? Similarly, if an institution mentions a need for a researcher in a specific area, they are doing so for a reason, and you should not assume that your great research in an unrelated area will suffice. For both teaching and research specialties, any claim that you fit the needs of the department should be backed up with experiences listed on your CV, otherwise the search committee will see your claims as empty.

Position Characteristics

Advertisements typically indicate position characteristics regarding tenure and rank. Most advertisements will explicitly point out that a position is tenure-track, often in the first sentence. If it is not clearly stated, however, you can look for certain indicators of non–tenure-track positions. Indications of how long the position lasts suggests a temporary position. For example, there may be language such as "a 1-year renewable contract" or "a 2-year position." Being on a 12- or 9-month contract, however, is not an indication of a temporary position. Rather, those terms indicate how salary is paid out or whether there are expectations for summer work.

Rank is another indicator of a position being on the tenure track. Advertisements for an *assistant professor* indicate a tenure-track, entry-level position that is open to candidates with degrees or who are finishing up their degrees. Position titles of *instructor, lecturer, adjunct,* and *visiting* suggest a position off the tenure track. Remember that the faculty position types can override institution type; instructors, lecturers, and adjuncts positions always emphasize teaching, no matter the institution. One added complexity is that community colleges' use of position titles does not always follow these conventions, so do not eliminate positions at community colleges on the basis of title alone.

Some advertisements will mention that the position is for an "open rank," and this indicates that the search committee is willing to consider hiring both new and experienced faculty. Yes, this means someone in graduate school might be competing with a full professor for the same position. From the grad school perspective, this hardly seems fair. Indeed, some institutions, mainly those of the elite and research-intensive variety, are notorious for poaching well-established professors rather than hiring and promoting new faculty. For the most part, however, search committees for positions of all types adjust their evaluations of CVs based on where candidates are in their professional careers.

METHODS FOR INVESTIGATING JOBS

Advertisements make every school sound like a shining educational beacon, but some are filthy diploma mills. You should do some research before applying for positions to ensure that you are not wasting your time on the dirty players in the educational market. Or, less dramatically, do some research to ensure that a position is as good of a fit as it seems in the idealized advertisement.

College websites can be a source of obvious and not-so-obvious information about positions. Of course, there will be information about the psychology program, faculty, and curriculum. Dig a little deeper, however, and some more obscure trends will emerge. To get a sense of scholarly rigor, look on individual faculty webpages to assess the recency of research publications and projects. In addition, see how many faculty members have links to laboratory webpages and what facilities seem to be associated with the labs. Most colleges make their course enrollment data public, and this represents a wealth of information about faculty responsibilities and program health. Looking at course data will illustrate how many courses faculty typically teach, who teaches what, how much of the curriculum is taught by adjuncts, class sizes, and what topics are popular and unpopular.

Nearly all job advertisements make claims about commitment to diversity, but college websites can indicate just how much institutions follow through with those claims. The demographic makeup of students, faculty, and administrators provides one indication of the climate for individuals from diverse backgrounds (American Psychological Association, n.d.-b; Boyd et al., 2017). Candidates can search for evidence of programming specifically designed to increase the success of diverse students and faculty. If diversity or cultural programming on campus seems less than ideal, websites will also contain evidence about initiatives and strategic plans designed to improve the campus climate.

Colleges' tight management of their websites ensures that they only include positive information, but heading "off campus" to unaffiliated websites can provide both objective and subjective data about an institution. If you are having a hard time getting a sense of the research culture in a department, one solution is to look up the faculty members using an author search in PsycINFO, Web of Science, Google Scholar, or another metric-producing website. The typical number of publications and citations in a department will be helpful in determining the expectations for research productivity. Trends in publication are useful as well. Do faculty have early-career publications and few thereafter? Is there a clear rift in publication rates among more recent hires and people who have been there since Freud's bar mitzvah? Trends that indicate shifts in research emphasis or support should be investigated further.

Any institution that receives federal money via student financial aid, which is virtually all of them, must provide the government with piles of data that are then made freely available on the Internet. The College Navigator (https://nces.ed.gov/collegenavigator/) and College Scorecard (https://collegescorecard.ed.gov/) are both government websites designed to help potential students learn about and compare institutions, but they work just as well for potential faculty. Entrance exam sores, graduation rates, campus security, earnings after graduation, accreditation status—these are just some of the pieces of information found on these websites that can give a sense of the school's standing in relation to peer institutions.

The government websites provide objective (relatively speaking) information about institutions, but plenty of subjective information can be found as well. Too many publications and news outlets to name here profit from evaluating and ranking colleges, and this can be valuable information about an institution's reputation. If you want to hear the students' side of things, check out Ratemyprofessors.com to see how prospective colleges, departments, and faculty stack up in the classroom. Moving on to straight-up gossip, the Academic Job Wiki provides links to where candidates can share their opinions, including dedicated webpages for calling out "Universities to Fear" and "Universities to Love." Reader beware. Finally, talk to your mentors and people in your broader professional network to get a sense of the quality of institutions and programs.

Before closing out this section, we must deal with the great boogeyman of job searches: the inside candidate. Researching a position may produce evidence of a candidate who seems to have an inside advantage—the visiting professor, the alum, the spouse, the frequent coauthor. There is no denying that inside candidates may have an advantage, especially at community colleges where internal hires are common (Fals-Stewart, 1996; Twombly, 2005). Nonetheless, the inside candidate may have offers elsewhere, the pool of outside candidates may be better than the inside candidate, or the perceived inside candidate may have already spoiled his or her chances in some way. There are just too many factors at play in a faculty search for it ever to be a foregone conclusion due to an inside candidate (Vick et al., 2016). So, if the position fits, apply.

IT'S ALL ABOUT FIT

It all comes down to fit between you and the position. If I could go back and give my graduate school self one piece of job-search advice, it would be to apply only for jobs that matched my teaching and research interests. There is no way to tell what a search committee's standards will be when evaluating applicants, but it is safe to assume that they will closely match the preferences as stated in the job advertisement. So, be honest with yourself and narrow down your potential jobs to those for which you think the committee will agree that you are a good fit. Moreover, after all that time, effort, and expense pursuing a degree in psychology, do you really want to take any old job, regardless of whether it matches your passions? Not everyone is in the privileged position to hold out for the best fitting job, but if you have the option, take it.

When deciding if a position is a good enough fit to warrant an application, ask yourself questions about the position's potential effect on your research, teaching, and lifestyle. Some important research-based questions include the following:

- Do your research record and long-term research agenda match the faculty in terms frequency of publications and quality of outlets?

- Will you be able to do your research given the local resources?
- Will the teaching load allow enough time for you to maintain a program of research?
- If you need grants to support your research, will you be able to mount a serious funding campaign if you are at the institution?

More teaching-minded questions are as follows:

- Would the value you place on teaching fit in the department?
- Does your preferred pedagogical style fit with the typical class size and format?
- Do the courses associated with the position seem interesting enough that you want to teach them, perhaps every semester, for the foreseeable future?
- Are you excited to work with the type of students who attend the college?

Finally, there are lifestyle questions:

- Can you see yourself living in the area?
- Is the location close enough to (or far enough away from) your family?
- Is the location amenable to dependents or partners who will be moving with you?
- Will you be proud to tell colleagues where you work?
- Does it seem like you will find support in the community?

In conclusion, keep in mind the delicate balancing act required of the job seeker: Do not ask for a job that you would not accept, but do not close yourself off from career opportunities that might be rewarding in unexpected ways.

5 WRITING A CURRICULUM VITAE

Curriculum vitae (CVs) offer no place to hide. The only way to build an impressive CV is through accomplishment. Thus, virtually every job application at 4-year institutions requires a CV (Clifton & Buskist, 2005). No matter how strong applicants make themselves out to be in their other application materials, if the CV does not back up those claims, an application will not move forward. Because of its importance, the CV gets its own chapter, and what follows is advice and strategies for making sure that your CV increases your chances of moving forward in the search process.

As is often the case, things work a little differently at community colleges, where job advertisements sometimes allow applicants to submit a CV or a résumé. Many of the details in a CV are irrelevant in demonstrating to community college search committees that you can teach, which is the one thing they need to know. Thus, some experts suggest submitting a résumé rather than a CV to community colleges (Jenkins, 2003). If you decide to take that approach, I suggest creating a CV first to ensure that you have a complete record of your academic accomplishments and then summarizing it in the form of résumé with the help of your university's career center. Advisors and other

http://dx.doi.org/10.1037/0000152-006
Becoming a Psychology Professor: Your Guide to Landing the Right Academic Job,
by G. A. Boysen

mentors, long used to the academic CV, will have less insight than people working at the career center on how to create a tight, attractive résumé.

TYPICAL CV CONTENT

A well-crafted CV should make a good first impression and withstand scrutiny after the first cursory round of screening. How to do this is a bit of a mystery because, with a few exceptions, CVs have resisted standardization, and there are no strict rules regarding content, organization, or formatting. Where is the American Psychological Association *Publication Manual* when you really need it? Nonetheless, experts have provided some excellent recommendations that you can use as a starting point for creating your CV (Kelsky, 2015; Kuther, 2008; Morgan & Landrum, 2012; Vick, Furlong, & Lurie, 2016). An important step after you have a draft of your CV is to get as many people as possible, preferably individuals with experience evaluating job candidates, to examine it and give you their opinions. You do not have follow every person's idiosyncratic preferences ("You must use a serif font!"), but make changes when a consensus emerges about faults ("You must not include martial arts training!").

Contact Information

The first section of the CV is the most standardized. Everyone's CV starts with their name, typically in larger and bolder font, and professional contact information including email, phone number, and mailing address. A professional webpage link or social media handle may also be provided. To add a clear air of professionalism, try to provide only contact information that is associated with an academic institution. Leave off all nonprofessional information.

Basic Credentials

The basic credentials section contains education, employment history, and professional licensure or certification. Under an "Education" heading, list all of your degrees, the institutions, and years of graduation. For your advanced degrees, list the thesis and dissertation titles and the faculty member who chaired your committees. Graduation honors are typically listed with degrees.

"Professional Experience" comes next, and this section can be broken down into subsections if necessary: postdoctoral positions, fellowships, clinical internships, academic appointments, and so on. For professional positions, list titles, institutions, and dates; this is not a résumé, so omit other details about the work. In general, because CVs are a record of a person's professional life, only employment and positions since the start of your psychology education need to be listed. Believe me, no one needs to know about the summers you spent flipping burgers, cleaning monkey cages, or washing windows in college (my real summer jobs by the way). Finally, people in specializations where licensure or other specialized credentials are pertinent can note them under their own heading with relevant information such as the licensing body and number.

Most CVs present contact information and basic credentials in that order, but from that point forward, the sections of CVs, their organization, and their extensiveness vary according to the focus of a psychologist's career.

Research Experience

A perfectly respectable CV requires only two sections in the research experience section: "Publications" and "Presentations." List publications in order by year. Because peer-reviewed journal publications are the most revered research product in psychology, list them first. A useful organizational strategy is to create a new subsection once you have multiple instances of one specific type of research product. For example, presentations might eventually be broken up into categories such as "Poster Presentations," "Symposiums," and "Local Presentations." For people looking to work at baccalaureate colleges and master's institutions, indicating undergraduate coauthors serves as a signal that you value research mentorship.

One dilemma faced by job applicants, especially those who are early in their careers, is how to address unpublished manuscripts in the CV. Some people include "In Preparation" and "Under Review" sections for their unpublished manuscripts, and having these sections is one way to demonstrate a program of research in which there are manuscripts in the pipeline for publication. Nonetheless, everyone knows that having research in preparation or under review are not guarantees of publication, and search committees will not count any line of research on a CV that is not in press or in print. Furthermore, a long list of manuscripts that are not accepted for publication conveys an image of a researcher who unable to close the deal on publications.

At doctoral institutions, receiving external funding to support research can be as much of job requirement as publication. As such, faculty at doctoral institutions will sometimes put a "Grants" section before their publications; after all, many types of research cannot be carried out, let alone published, without funding. The "Grants" section should list individual grants in order by date, and each entry should include the amount, names of investigators, funding agency, and title of the project. Do not be afraid to start small with listing grants. Keep track of small grants for travel to conferences or to fund small research projects because they provide evidence that you are an active scholar whose work is worth funding.

Some other research sections frequently make their way into CVs, but they are less essential than the objective research accomplishments already covered. Some include a summary section called "Research Interests" and may even place it before their publications. The advantage to such a section is that it can provide a frame of reference for understanding the connection between publications and can suggest a coherent program of research. Sections such as "Research Skills" and "Research Experience" can add some valuable information about scholarly interests and abilities. There are downsides to including these sections and their variants, and the biggest is the potential for search committees to see them as padding. Another problem is that CVs should show, not tell. Rather than telling readers that you have research interests, skills, and experiences, show them with your academic positions, publications, and presentations.

Teaching Experience

Once again, a perfectly respectable CV requires only the simplest information about teaching experiences. For the typical graduate student, only two sections are necessary: "Courses Taught" and "Teaching Assistantships." Just as publications are the most important part of the research section, "Courses Taught" is the most important part of the teaching section. No amount of experience as a TA or guest lecturer is equivalent to having full responsibility for one course. For all courses taught, list the names of classes at minimum, but details such as enrollment, level (i.e., course number), and semesters taught can also be added. If it is not obvious from your employment history, also indicate the institution where the course was offered. Include a separate "Teaching Assistantships" sections using the same format.

If you have not had the opportunity to teach courses in your specialty area, which is not an uncommon experience in graduate programs, you can use a "Teaching Interests" section to list the courses that you are qualified to teach. However, interests are not accomplishments, and the courses will not count the same as ones you have taught. Also, remember that application materials will include a cover letter and perhaps a teaching philosophy in which you can address teaching interests.

Service

The "Service" section follows many of the previously outlined rules. Organize service by year to demonstrate a consistent pattern of engagement. Start with one section, and then break it up as you have enough departmental, university, professional, and community service to warrant separate sections. Entries for individual service experiences should provide your position or title, the title of the project, and the organization.

Professional Engagement

Several CV sections can demonstrate engagement with psychology as a profession and an ongoing commitment to growth. "Professional Affiliation" is a standard CV section; it simply lists memberships in professional organizations. Entries should list the organization name and, perhaps, the dates of membership. A less common section is "Professional Development," but it can be useful for highlighting skills and training not otherwise reflected in the education section. To illustrate, the section might list seminars on advanced statistical techniques, attendance at conferences, or workshops on pedagogy.

Applied Experience

The most obvious applied experience psychologists will have is placements in clinical positions. A "Clinical Experience" section demonstrates expertise and ability to teach, train, and supervise others in your field. For accredited degree programs, clinical experience may be required for faculty, so applicants seeking jobs in such programs will want to create a separate section for those activities. Entries in this section should include position dates, title, and the agency. For clinicians and nonclinicians, any work performed as a consultant, paid or unpaid, is another applied experience to list on the CV.

Recognitions

If others have officially recognized your work as outstanding in some way, include it in your CV. An "Honors and Awards" section is standard. In fact, some value this section so highly, they place it right after "Education" so that it supersedes all other accomplishments. A less formal type of recognition is attention from the media. Among research-minded psychologists, including a "Media Coverage" section illustrates the impact of scholarship and its funding potential.

ORGANIZATIONAL STRATEGIES

With the potential for a dozen or more sections in a CV, finding the proper order for them can be tricky, but there are some rules to follow (Kelsky, 2015; Morgan & Landrum, 2012; Vick et al., 2016). To begin, the contact information and basic credentials go first without exception; not having that information first or including other information in those spots will make you stand out, but not in a good way. Next, you have a choice to make: teaching or research?

Search committees will primarily be evaluating you on teaching and research, so there is no reason to bury these sections in your CV. The choice of putting teaching or research first is institution-dependent—place teaching and research in the order the institution you are applying to values them. Prioritization can be determined by considering what type of institution it is, looking at the order and emphasis of teaching and research in the job ad, and by doing some online research on what the CVs of current faculty look like at the institution. In the unlikely event of a tie, put your most impressive qualification first.

Another useful organizational principle is to put more prestigious accomplishments before less prestigious accomplishments. When considering scholarship, peer-reviewed work is valued above all else, so put that material first (Kelsky, 2015). A typical order of sections would be "Journal Articles," "Conference Presentations," and "Local Presentations." Similarly, competitive national grants would go before local grants. Although there is not a system of peer review to guide the organization of sections on teaching, "Courses Taught" is most important and should always go first. Other teaching-related experiences and professional development should follow in that order.

HOW SEARCH COMMITTEES AT DIFFERENT INSTITUTIONS READ CVS

Motivation affects perception. Stand at the bottom of a hill, and it will seem steeper than when you are standing at the top contemplating an easy descent. A sumptuous dinner tastes better on an empty stomach than if you overate at lunch. Search committees have motivations too that are based on their desire to hire a specific type of faculty member. Take the CVs of the number-one job candidate at a doctoral university and at a baccalaureate college, then switch the search committee doing the evaluation; neither candidate would make the short list at the other type of school. This is not a bad thing. Everyone benefits when search committees recruit candidates who are a good fit for a position.

Because search committees at different types of institutions have different motivations and preferences, experts agree that you must tailor your CV to each type of institution (Kelsky, 2015; Vick et al., 2016). Examples of CVs that are research- and teaching-focused can be found on this book's companion website (http://pubs.apa.org/books/supp/boysen/). One of the first things search committees will look for is the order in which applicants place teaching and research sections in a CV, and failure to conform to their expected order, although not a fatal flaw, may raise immediate concern about fit with the position (Boysen, Morton, & Nieves, in press). If a candidate is applying to different types of institutions, the order of teaching and research sections can easily be swapped, but the switch in emphasis must be consistent across all application materials, especially the cover letter, or the search committee will notice the mixed message. Although creating different versions of your CV, one that is teaching focused and one that is research focused, is a sound strategy, if you find yourself making such a switch, consider whether the jobs you are applying to all fit your career interests and goals.

Search committees at doctoral universities will examine CVs for evidence of candidates' potential to be productive and influential scholars. Fit is always most important, so they will examine whether training, publications, and interests match the field of research mentioned in the job advertisement. Numbers matter too. They will be counting publications. Not all publications are equivalent at doctoral universities, however, and high-impact journals are the expected outlet for research. Having publications in low-impact journals, regardless of number or the actual quality of the research, can count against a candidate. Publications and grants should demonstrate the existence of an independent and coherent program of research. Too many secondary coauthorships or too many papers with an advisor suggest an absence of independence. Having a grant is not required, but search committees will place value on a record of attempts to secure funding. Finally, prestige has its influence. The presence of famous mentors, elite programs, highly competitive postdocs, and coveted awards all send the message that a candidate has a bright future in research.

Baccalaureate college search committees will be looking primarily at teaching potential. The number of previous courses taught is an important indication of candidates' potential, but the experiences must fit the needs of the department. Experienced teachers who cannot teach the required courses will not be hired. For less experienced candidates, search committees will give minor consideration to teaching assistantships, especially if the courses match up with those listed in the job advertisement. Guest lectures carry no weight. Although teaching experience of all types is valued, search committees will be especially looking for evidence that candidates have taught smaller classes. Evidence of pedagogical training and service related to teaching will also factor into evaluations. Research still matters at baccalaureate colleges, but the standard for performance at all but the most elite institutions is consistent engagement rather than prolific publication in high-impact journals. What search committees will also look for in research, however, is evidence of undergraduate engagement and potential for students to make meaningful contributions, perhaps even as coauthors.

Community college search committees are looking for evidence that a candidate can teach, and the other CV or résumé sections cannot make up for weakness in teaching. In fact, community colleges require several years of teaching experience for a candidate to receive serious consideration, so the CV or résumé must prioritize pedagogical experience above all else. The unique mission of community colleges does lead search committees to look for candidates who list a variety of courses in their teaching interests rather than a limited set of courses in a narrow specialty area. In addition, they are looking for lower level courses, especially introductory psychology, rather than upper level courses. Finally, students at community colleges are diverse, and search committees will be looking for experience or training that indicates a candidate's ability to teach students from various backgrounds and with various levels of college preparation.

As always, master's universities are in the middle due to their mixed identities. Some master's universities aspire to be doctoral universities. In such cases, search committees will examine CVs with the hope of hiring faculty whose research would not be out of place at a doctoral university. Other master's universities emphasize more of a teaching and research balance, and search committees would look down upon a CV demonstrating few teaching accomplishments. Overall, the best, albeit not very specific, advice is to pay close attention to the relative emphasis on teaching and research in job advertisements and on the departmental webpages and try to arrange your CV in a way that strikes a similar balance.

Things are different for adjunct and instructor positions. These positions are all about teaching no matter the institution type. The central issue is your ability to cover the courses listed in the job advertisement. Thus, the people doing the hiring will evaluate CVs based on teaching expertise and experience.

THE CV AS A 30-SECOND ADVERTISEMENT ABOUT YOU

In an episode of the TV show *The Office*, the world's worst boss Michael Scott must cut costs with a layoff, and the employees, recognizing Scott's capriciousness, try desperately to keep him happy, knowing that he will probably fire "the first person to give him a dirty look in the hall." Write your CV as if Michael Scott will be reviewing it, looking to get rid of anyone who gives him the slightest reason to do so. Such advice is not flattering to search committees, but it is realistic. In the early stages of screening applicants, search committee members do not read CVs carefully or completely because they are just looking to throw out inappropriate candidates (Lord, 2004; Vick et al., 2016). To make it past the first cursory scan for rejects, it is essential to make your CV into an advertisement for your strengths as a candidate.

Here is a test of your CV's utility as an advertisement. Take 30 seconds to flip through it reading only the headings and scanning the years of things listed under those headings. If you cannot glean in 30 seconds who you are, what your background is, the consistency of your academic record, and how much you emphasize teaching versus research, then it is time to revise because search committees will have the same difficulty. Give your CV to peers and mentors so that they can put it through the same test. Be sure that your CV sends a clear message to search committee members that you are a good fit for the position and that they should carefully consider the rest of your materials.

6 APPLICATION MATERIALS AND THE APPLICATION PROCESS

I have read hundreds of applications for faculty positions over the years, some of them quite remarkable. There was the cover letter that was a Unabomber-style manifesto outlining the transgressions of various college administrators, and there was the candidate who provided a link to a teaching demonstration on YouTube that was so comically bad, I still suspect it was someone's audition tape for *Saturday Night Live*. The materials of the people we eventually hired were remarkable too, but in a positive way. Often within a few paragraphs, candidates had transformed themselves from a stranger to someone I was happily imagining in the office next door.

Applicants for faculty positions have just a few short documents to make their case for being hired. As outlined in the previous chapter, the curriculum vitae (CV) is universally required as part of materials to be submitted, but applications almost as frequently require a cover letter (Clifton & Buskist, 2005; Murray, 2013). The purpose of cover letters is for applicants to introduce themselves and outline why they are a good candidate for the position. Self-proclamations are not enough, however, and letters of reference are also a standard part of application packages (Clifton & Buskist, 2005;

http://dx.doi.org/10.1037/0000152-007
Becoming a Psychology Professor: Your Guide to Landing the Right Academic Job,
by G. A. Boysen

Murray, 2013). This triumvirate—CV, cover letter, references—is the key to making the short list for interviews.

Depending on the position and the type of institution, search committees also use a few other materials to evaluate candidates (Clifton & Buskist, 2005; Murray, 2013). Research and teaching statements are both opportunities for candidates to outline their approaches to these professional activities in greater detail than a cover letter allows. Some institutions require teaching evaluations or "evidence of teaching effectiveness" to augment or replace the teaching statement. A newer, and still relatively uncommon, addition to application materials is the diversity statement, and it is a way for applicants to demonstrate a commitment to inclusivity in their work.

Procedures for evaluating these application materials are as diverse as the faculty members who make up search committees, but there are three typical steps in the process. First, each search committee member will look over application materials individually to form a list of top candidates. Depending on the committee, this first step may involve detailed guidelines for evaluation, or it may be a free-for-all in which each committee member implements evaluation criteria known only to them, and maybe not even to them. Second, the committee will come together and compare their top candidates. Third, discussion will occur with the goal of producing a short list of candidates for the first round of interviews. The discussion may be collegial or contentious, democratic or dictatorial, effortless or excruciating—but no discussion is necessary when the same candidate appears on everyone's list. Your goal is to be that candidate.

How does a job applicant become the candidate that everyone agrees on? Mostly, the person gathers professional experiences as outlined earlier in this book, but even candidates with exceptional records can be rejected. One reason for rejection is lack of attention to the subtle art and unstated rules of writing compelling application materials. This chapter outlines the craft and customs that produce materials worthy of the short list.

THE COVER LETTER: AN ABSTRACT OF YOUR FIT WITH THE POSITION

Picture yourself starting a literature review and using PsycINFO to find articles. Once you have put in a search term and clicked submit, you must weed through results full of false alarms to find sources that fit the scope of your review. Some titles look promising, but before making the time investment of reading the whole article, you scan the abstract to determine if the article's main message matches your needs. Search committees have a similar task. They have to weed through dozens of people who are not serious contenders for a position and select the few who match. Some candidates are eliminated by their title alone, but committee members read on for other candidates. Will they make the time investment of interviewing you? It largely depends on whether the committee members like the abstract you have constructed in your cover letter.

Cover Letter Content

The content of cover letters is person- and position-specific, but there are some common goals that job candidates should try to achieve. Experts emphasize three goals: establish fit, demonstrate knowledge about the position, and maintain a consistent message (Brems, Lampman, & Johnson, 1995; Morgan & Landrum, 2012; Morphew, Ward, & Wolf-Wendel, 2016; Vick, Furlong, & Lurie, 2016; Wells, Schofield, Clerkin, & Sheets, 2013). The first goal is to establish fit with the position requirements. Although search committee members can glean candidates' fit with a position through close examination of CVs, their cover letters should simplify the task by outlining a point-by-point argument for how their qualifications match the position requirements.

One strategy for evaluating your argument for fit is to make a list of every requirement and characteristic mentioned in the job advertisement and use it as a checklist for your cover letter. Too many boxes left unchecked is a sign of either a poor match with the position or a cover letter than needs some fine-tuning. If you are missing a major qualification but still think that you are a good fit, use the cover letter to address the issue rather than hoping that the search committee will miss it (Brems et al., 1995). Search committees may overlook a flaw that candidates reasonably explain, but having a flaw and the lack of foresight to acknowledge it is grounds for rejection.

The second goal for cover letters is to demonstrate knowledge about the department and college. A generic cover letter is a kiss of death (Boysen, Morton, & Nieves, in press; Landrum & Clump, 2004); it signals either indifference or indolence. Search committees are dominated by people who have a deep fondness for their work and for their college, so cover letters that express none of the same fondness will come off as apathetic at best and insulting at worst. One method for demonstrating knowledge is to find features and opportunities of genuine interest on departmental and college websites and then incorporate them into the letter. As with any writing technique, the effectiveness is all in the execution. Be sure that personalized touches come off as natural and not as false, fawning, or stalkerish.

Another method for demonstrating knowledge is to acknowledge the mission of the institution (Brakke, 2014; H. L. Miller, Flores, & Tait, 2014). Some knowledge of the mission will emerge naturally while outlining fit with the position requirements. Letters for doctoral universities will naturally focus on research, and letters to community colleges will naturally focus on teaching. However, cover letters should also acknowledge more unique aspects of mission. Small colleges, religious colleges, and colleges that serve specific populations stand out as examples where institutional identity must be addressed in some way. An excellent example is Spelman College, which is a historically Black college for women in Atlanta, Georgia; it is difficult to fathom an applicant being successful without acknowledging this doubly unique mission (Brakke, 2014). In the case of small liberal arts colleges, search committees value candidates who understand what college life is like in such a setting, and candidates should briefly highlight their experience with and interest in such colleges (Ault, 2014). Familiarity with the mission of a college is not enough to get you hired, but it will increase perception of you as having serious interest in the position.

The third and final goal for the cover letter is maintaining a consistent message about strengths and fit with the position. Although the details in the cover letter will meander a bit, the main message of who you are as a candidate must remain constant, and it is essential that the message be tailored to fit the institution. The message for doctoral universities is that you are an innovative and productive scholar. The message for community colleges is that you are a passionate and effective teacher. For master's universities and liberal arts colleges, the message is that you are both an effective teacher and a productive scholar—the relative weight placed on teaching and research will vary by institution.

Moving beyond broad goals, there are some additional rules to follow when selecting cover letter content. The focus so far has been on what to include, but there are also things that should be left out. Under no circumstances should a cover letter express negativity about students, colleagues, college policies, Mondays, the size of airline seats, the weather, or anything else (Boysen et al., in press). Keep the tone exclusively positive because nobody wants to hire a crank. Leave out personal material not directly relevant to your interest in or qualifications for the position (Boysen et al., in press; Brems et al., 1995; Morgan & Landrum, 2012). Search committees will view irrelevant personal information as a sign of ignorance or poor professional boundaries.

Irrelevant personal revelations are dangerous, but relevant ones can be beneficial. Because faculty members want to diversify their ranks, candidates may choose to reveal their personal experiences with diversity (Boyd et al., 2017). Also, if you have a personal connection to an area or an institution, mentioning it conveys a genuine interest in the position; however, it should be one sentence, not a main argument, of your cover letter. Placing too much emphasis on location as a reason for applying is a kiss of death (Boysen et al., in press). "I am relocating to Cambridge in the fall, thus I am applying for your open position at Harvard"—this argument sounds just as silly outside of the Ivy League. Finally, if search committee members will be suspicious, or merely unsure, about why you are leaving your current position, address the reason directly. When applying for my current position, it just so happened that I was also in my sixth year and applying for tenure, which is a time when some people flee intuitions in miserable failure. My interest moving was entirely family-based, so I included one straightforward sentence in my cover letter stating that family needs and not professional needs explained the timing of my job search. In summary, do not belabor professionally relevant revelations; establish credibility and move on to more pertinent credentials.

Cover Letter Format

One of life's great frustrations is ordering a Guinness and having it served in a vessel other than a proper pint glass (I may be exaggerating for effect here). Guinness simply does not taste as good served in anything else. Appearance matters in aesthetic enjoyment. There is a reason why performers wear elaborate costumes, why fancy restaurants use good silver, and why vinyl sounds better than digital. Likewise, format matters with your cover letter.

The most fraught formatting issue is length. Search committees read cover letters of dramatically different lengths (Brems et al., 1995; Schmaling, Trevino, Lind, Blume, & Baker, 2015). In one study, the number of lines of text in applicants' cover letters ranged from 4 to 150 (Brems et al., 1995). Four lines—can you imagine?

Dear Search Committee Members,

You have a job. I want a job. I teach. I research. My work is good. People like me. Please hire me.

Sincerely,

Dr. I. M. Tersely

Keeping in mind the need to provide a strong argument for fit and the limited patience of search committees, a rule of thumb is to keep letters under two single-spaced pages (Huang-Pollock & Mikami, 2007; Wells et al., 2013). Two pages is a good compromise. The length will offend neither those individuals who view one page as cursory nor those who view three pages as hubris.

The next most fraught issue is letterhead or no letterhead. Graduate students may not have easy access to letterhead, and there is room for debate about the ethics of using the resources of your current employer to seek a different employer. But think back to that pint of Guinness. Your letter will be more pleasing if it looks good, so use letterhead (Kelsky, 2015). That being said, you do not need paper stock with letterhead printed on it; as communications increasingly go paperless, traditional paper stock is being replaced with electronic files containing letterhead inserted as an image.

All other formatting issues seem minor, but ensuring that your cover letter conforms to them will communicate professionalism and conscientiousness. Include a specific salutation rather than a "To whom it may concern" or "Dear Sirs and Madams." Addressing the letter to the chair of the search committee is appropriate, as is addressing it to "Search Committee Members." Do not address your letter to a person who is not part of hiring decision, such as the human resources representative or a faculty secretary. Specify the position being applied for in the first paragraph because there may be multiple searches occurring at the same time. Include the institution's address above the salutation, and double-check to make sure you have not accidentally left the wrong institution name somewhere in the letter. Everyone knows you are applying for different positions, but such a blatant reminder is a kiss of death (Boysen et al., in press). If it is not already in the letterhead, include contact information at the end by your name. Sign the letter.

Writing Suggestions for Cover Letters

So far, I have focused on the "what" of cover letters, but the "how" needs to be considered as well. Make no mistake: Cover letters are writing samples, and they should be treated with the same attention to writing process as any other important piece of work. Bad writing can lead to rejection (Boysen et al., in press). Courtesy of George Orwell (1954), here are the pithiest rules for good writing that you will ever find:

1. Never use a metaphor, simile, or other figure of speech which you are used to seeing in print.
2. Never use a long word where a short one will do.
3. If it is possible to cut a word out, always cut it out.
4. Never use the passive where you can use the active.

5. Never use a foreign phrase, a scientific word, or a jargon word if you can think of an everyday English equivalent.
6. Break any of these rules sooner than say anything outright barbarous. (p. 176)

Learn them, love them, and use them to edit your cover letter

Another famous writing dictum is to show, not tell. In other words, rather than telling readers "Freud was angry," show readers his anger by writing, "The air suddenly crackled with tension as Freud's face reddened and he leaned into Jung, ready for battle." Similarly, rather than telling readers that you are a good teacher and researcher, show them the evidence you have accumulated to back up those claims.

Finally, even successful writers need editors. Get as many eyes as possible on your cover letter (Morgan & Landrum, 2012). The plurality of perspectives is exactly what you face with a search committee, so make revisions that satisfy people with varied tastes. Plus, it becomes impossible to find every writing error in a document when you go through as many dafts [*sic*; see?] as you will with a cover letter.

An essential point to understand about cover letters is that, rather than providing objective list of accomplishments like a CV, they are arguments for fit with a position made by selectively emphasizing certain accomplishments from a CV. To help make that point, I have included four cover letters, all based on the same fictional CV, but written for positions at different institutions on this book's companion website (http://pubs.apa.org/books/supp/boysen/).

THE TEACHING STATEMENT AS AN EXPRESSION OF MODEL TEACHING

Cover letters are where applicants roll through the greatest hits of their careers without great detail, so search committees often request additional descriptions of candidates' approaches to teaching, research, and diversity. Teaching statements, also referred to as teaching philosophies, are required for about one third of positions (Benson & Buskist, 2005; Meizlish & Kaplan, 2008). Teaching statements serve a dual purpose: They provide a tool for search committees to evaluate applicants' approach to teaching, but requiring them also sends a message to potential applicants about the value placed on teaching at the institution.

Teaching philosophies should demonstrate careful thought about pedagogy that has resulted in intentional, well-founded teaching practices. They are somewhat more personal and informal than cover letters, but that does not mean that they should be confessional or devoid of structure. An easy way to produce a cogent teaching philosophy—and one that might be of real use to you as a teacher—is to follow one of the standard templates outlined in Table 6.1. Start by answering the questions as they apply to your approach to teaching and experiences in the classroom. Then, tie your answers together with strong transitions, perhaps an overarching theme, and introductory and concluding statements.

Within the broader structure of the teaching statement, candidates can make additional points that strengthen their case for fit with a position. Teaching statements for community and baccalaureate colleges should only mention undergraduate education. Community college instructors encounter a diverse set of students in their classroom, so emphasizing the ability to teach to different populations will be beneficial. For baccalaureate colleges, candidates will benefit from the infusion of information about advising, supervision of student research, general education courses, and research on teaching and learning (Brems et al., 1995; R. L. Miller, 2014; Morgan & Landrum, 2012; Troisi et al., 2014). At doctoral and master's universities, graduate mentorship can be incorporated, and, although the focus of the statement is supposedly on teaching, scholarship should remain a theme (Huang-Pollock & Mikami, 2007; Kelsky, 2015). Finally, one of the main

TABLE 6.1. Sample Templates for Teaching Statements

Template 1	Template 2	Template 3
• What are the positive effects of teaching? • What methods do you use to accomplish those positive effects? • What are some specific examples of the methods? • What is some evidence that the methods you used were effective?	• What values have led you to be committed to teaching? • What goals do you have for student learning? • To achieve your student learning goals, what teaching style and specific methods do you use? • How do you assess whether students are meeting learning goals? • What is your professional development plan to ensure that you stay fresh and improve as a teacher?	• How do people learn? • What is your role in that learning? • What are the specific ways you ensure that people learn in the classroom?

Note. Data from previous work (Kelsky, 2015; Morgan & Landrum, 2012).

things search committees will want to know about candidates is if they can cover courses mentioned in the advertisement, so the teaching statement may include a list of courses candidates are prepared to teach and ideas for new courses.

There is a lot to cover in a teaching statement, but avoid the temptation to produce a pedagogical tome. Although length recommendations range from one to three pages (Kelsky, 2015; Morgan & Landrum, 2012; Wells et al., 2013), remember that search committees have a lot of applications to read and will appreciate candidates who get to the point. Be sure that you have a point, however. Teaching statements are not the place to spout educational buzzwords, and they are not the place to be overly personal, sentimental, or, ironically enough, philosophical (Kelsky, 2015; Morgan & Landrum, 2012). Remember the dictum: show, not tell. Rather than telling search committees "I am passionate about teaching," show them that you are passionate about education by sharing specific practices and evidence. Sample teaching statements written to fit research- and teaching-focused positions can be found on this book's companion website (http://pubs.apa.org/books/supp/boysen/).

THE RESEARCH STATEMENT AS A SIGN OF PAST PRODUCTIVITY AND FUTURE POTENTIAL

As a good student of APA Style, you know that every paper needs to have an abstract. Imagine writing an abstract not just for one of your studies but for your entire research program—that is the essence of a research statement. They summarize what you study, why it is important, and what you will do next (Morgan & Landrum, 2012). Applications require research statements about as frequently as teaching statements (Benson & Buskist, 2005), but the chances of their being required increase with an institution's research emphasis. The essential task of a research statement is to establish past productivity and future potential.

The organization of research statements tends to follow a set structure: overview, description of the field, summary of current research, and future plans (Brems et al., 1995; Kelsky, 2015; Morgan & Landrum, 2012; Vick et al., 2016). The overview section serves as an introduction to your research area. In this section, describe the theme that organizes your research and provide enough of a summary that people who read only this first section will have a sense of what you do. Readers should know why your research is important from this section alone. Next, provide a description of your research field in terms that a nonexpert can understand. The purpose of this section is to demonstrate your expertise and show the logical line connecting past work to your own work.

The next, and arguably most important, section of a research statement is the summary of your current research. Use this section to outline ongoing research projects in some detail. Readers should have a good sense of what methods you use, your results, and your typical publication outlets. Just as important, however, is clearly establishing for the reader the ways in which your work is new and innovative. Emphasize your contributions to the field.

In the final section, establish your future research plans, including required resources and sources of funding. The main purpose of this section is to show that you have a coherent program of research with plans for future directions that are consistent with the college to which you are applying. Readers should believe that there is continuity in your research and that your lab will be up and running right away if hired. For students and recent graduates, the future research section is also essential for establishing the ability to do independent work.

Many types of institutions require research statements, everywhere from places where six-digit grants are the norm to places where every publication is celebrated as an achievement, and the statements should vary based on how research fits into the institutional mission. Example statements can be found on this book's companion website (http://pubs.apa.org/books/supp/boysen/). At research-focused doctoral and master's universities, relative to teaching-focused colleges, it is much more important to establish plans and potential for securing external funding. Supervision of graduate students at these institutions, particularly doctoral universities, is part of research responsibilities, and it is useful to outline plans for mentorship and running a lab. At some doctoral universities, accepting new graduate students may be contingent on finding external grants to fund them. Finally, because so much research is done collaboratively and research-focused institutions want to hire truly independent scholars, it is important to emphasize the ability to be productive as a self-directed researcher, not just as an acolyte or a collaborator.

Research is unlikely to be weighted first in the hiring process at baccalaureate colleges, so the research statement, when it is required, should be used to communicate a combined message about scholarship, teaching, and overall fit (Ault, 2014; Buddie, 2014; Critchfield & Jordan, 2014; Morgan & Landrum, 2012; Troisi, Christopher, & Batsell, 2014; Wells et al., 2013). Of utmost importance is establishing that your research will be relevant to undergraduates and that your work will afford undergraduates with meaningful experiences; this is also important at teaching-focused master's universities. Given the reduced research infrastructure at baccalaureate colleges, the statement should also emphasize the ability to implement a program of research with the available resources. If your research requires support that exceeds what the college can offer, then make it clear how you will access outside resources or establish research collaborations. As is the case in all application materials, establishing fit is the main goal, and search committees at baccalaureate colleges will reject even the most prolific scholars if they do not appreciate the appropriate role of scholarship at the institution.

The format of research statements is similar to that of teaching statements, but they can be longer (one–five pages) and are more likely to include figures and references (Huang-Pollock & Mikami, 2007; Morgan & Landrum, 2012). There will be nonspecialists on search committees, and perhaps even faculty outside of psychology, so make sure that your statement is comprehensible to a nonexpert (Vick et al., 2016). Despite the lure of discipline-specific jargon, remember that the statement is about more than your research; it is also about your ability to effectively communicate about your research.

OTHER APPLICATION MATERIALS AND WHAT THEY MEAN

The most common job application materials have a fairly standard format. Search committees and applicants know what a CV or a research statement should look like. Other, less common application materials lack such shared understanding. Requests for student evaluations, evidence of teaching effectiveness, and diversity statements can be addressed in many ways, but what follows are some suggestions for putting together these more ambiguous application materials.

Student Evaluations

Student evaluations are a common tool used by search committees to evaluate candidates' teaching effectiveness (Benson & Buskist, 2005; Brems et al., 1995; Meizlish & Kaplan, 2008). Some search committees may want raw data, and others will want summaries. Although there is no standard format for presenting student evaluations for review, Table 6.2 illustrates a recommended format for summarizing means (Boysen, 2016; Franklin, 2001). Just as in research, data is uninterpretable without context, so provide statistical information such as comparison means, measures of variance, and,

TABLE 6.2. Format for Presenting Mean Teaching Evaluation Summaries

Course	Semester	Enrollment/ responded	Ratings of overall instructor effectiveness		Comparison mean: Overall instructor rating for my college		Statistical comparison
			M	SD	M	SD	
PSY 115	F 17	100/87	4.14	0.45	4.07	0.53	Not significantly different
PSY 201	S 17	50/45	4.66	0.35	4.07	0.53	Significantly higher
PSY 202	F 18	50/44	4.01	0.49	4.07	0.53	Not significantly different

Note. Ratings occurred on a scale from 1 (*extremely ineffective*) to 5 (*extremely effective*).

if you are a real go-getter, statistical comparisons. Presenting some statistical tests is particularly relevant if your means are below average but not significantly so. Also, provide the response rate to indicate the representativeness of the sample and to illustrate that you encourage student feedback.

Open-ended comments are dangerous—both to the ego and to landing a job. Providing unfiltered student comments risks search committees over-interpreting any negative feedback as a sign of poor teaching, but search committees also might dismiss candidates who provide only glowing comments as transparently manipulative. If you decide to include comments, the solution is to follow the same principle as with the qualitative data: Analyze the comments and provide summary data (Boysen, 2016; Lewis, 2001; Richmond, Boysen, & Gurung, 2016). The method illustrated in Table 6.3 is one approach to qualitative analysis that lets you select which aspects of teaching you want to emphasize; these become the left-hand column of teaching characteristics. After defining the relevant characteristics, go through your evaluation comments and count the number of them that affirm the characteristics or provide you with direction for improvement. Analyzing and organizing comments in this way gives you control over what teaching skills you want to emphasize, and it shows, once again, that you take student feedback seriously.

Evidence of Teaching Effectiveness

Search committees are most likely to evaluate candidates' teaching effectiveness by requesting student evaluations, but a more general request for "evidence of teaching effectiveness" suggests that they want to see something more than evaluations. Few applications will require a full teaching

TABLE 6.3. Presenting Summaries of Teaching Evaluation Comments

Teaching characteristic	Affirming comments (n)	Improvement comments (n)
Enthusiastic	• Seems to love psych (8) • Has fun (5) • Engaging discussion (5)	• Lectures can be dull (3)
Organized	• Organized notes (20) • Clear syllabus (5)	• Gets off topic sometimes (7)
Open/fair	• Helpful (20) • Answers questions (6)	• Tests too hard (9) • Grades on papers unclear (4)
Knowledgeable	• Knows topic (25)	• Does not always know answers to questions (3)
Skilled	• Good speaker (8)	• Needs to lead discussion better (10)

portfolio (Benson & Buskist, 2005); they are too long and cumbersome. Nonetheless, content from teaching portfolios can be cannibalized to produce a condensed teaching effectiveness document.

Teaching portfolios often contain products created by the teacher, evaluations of teaching, and products created by the students (Franz et al., 2014; Morgan & Landrum, 2012; Wells et al., 2013). Teaching products can include anything that you have created for your teaching or to describe your teaching: a teaching statement, a list of courses taught, syllabi, course materials, ideas for new courses, and examples of how you use student feedback or assessment to make pedagogical changes. Evaluations of teaching include any outside description of your pedagogical work: student evaluations, peer or mentor observations, teaching certificates and awards, and student testimonials. Finally, products of student work consist of student accomplishments stemming from your teaching: sample assignments, descriptions of student achievements, and products from mentorship such as publications.

Creating a short document outlining evidence of teaching effectiveness from the long list of materials that make up a teaching portfolio will take a heroic culling effort. The most important items from a job application standpoint are the teaching statement, student evaluations, syllabi, and course list (Franz et al., 2014; Kelsky, 2015; Wells et al., 2013). Beyond these essentials, try to match any additional content with institutional emphasis. For example, search committees at community colleges and baccalaureate colleges will be impressed by individual student mentoring and evidence of student engagement and success. Search committees at doctoral and master's universities will be impressed by integration of scholarship with teaching and evidence of being a productive research mentor.

Diversity Statements

The newest addition to the standard job application package is a diversity statement. Because of the requirement's novelty, no standard format has emerged (Schmaling et al., 2015; Vick et al., 2016). However, their basic purpose is to see if candidates are aware of the experiences of people from diverse backgrounds in higher education, especially the difficulties they face, and to have candidates explain how they ensure equal access to all students (Kelsky, 2015).

Candidates can write about many topics to demonstrate the infusion of diversity in their work (Kelsky, 2015; Schmaling et al., 2015; Sikorski & Bruce, 2014). The diversity statement is ultimately about a candidate's ability to work with people from various backgrounds, so one topic to address is experience teaching and mentoring diverse students. Fostering appreciation for diversity among other people is also valuable, so candidates could discuss the ways they infuse diversity into their teaching through course topics, assignments, or activities. Many psychologists' research emphasizes topics related to diversity, and this can be highlighted. Finally, candidates may disclose personal diversity if they so choose (Schmaling et al., 2015). This type of personal revelation is appropriate, but it requires careful consideration of the potential ways it might help or hurt the chances of getting an interview (Kelsky, 2015; Vick et al., 2016).

SECURING MEANINGFUL LETTERS OF RECOMMENDATION

Obtaining a faculty position requires candidates to secure positive letters of recommendation. Failure at this task can be catastrophic. Consider the job candidate whose application file contained the following recommendation letter.

Dear _____,

_____ has asked me to provide a letter of support for his application for a position in your department.

Sincerely, _____

I doubt he got an interview.

Who is to blame for such a letter? A strong case can be made that faculty members should decline to write letters they know will be negative, but job candidates are ultimately responsible for ensuring the strength of their application package, and this includes letters of recommendation. Search committees treat these letters as one of the most important aspects of the application (Benson & Buskist, 2005; Ng, 1997; Sheehan & Haselhorst, 1999). It does not even take a negative recommendation letter to be rejected; even lukewarm letters can be a kiss of death (Boysen et al., in press). Thus, one of the essential tasks of graduate school is to find three to five people whom you trust to write a letter of recommendation that contains positive and detailed information about your professional abilities and collegiality.

Once you have made an official decision to go on the job market, make a list of the people who are potential letter writers. Assuming that you are still in graduate school or just graduated, at the very top of that list, without exception, should be your graduate advisor. The expectation that a letter is forthcoming from candidates' advisors is so strong that its absence can tank an application (Boysen et al., in press). Thus, if your advisor cannot or should not serve as a reference due to death, disagreement, or degeneracy, have at least one other letter writer explain the situation (Wells et al., 2013). As with cover letters, potential flaws in an application are forgivable if they are acknowledged, but ignoring them is a kiss of death. Only when applying for jobs several years after earning your degree is a letter from your advisor is no longer mandatory.

Next on your list of references are the three to four faculty members who know you best (Darley & Zanna, 2004), and this can be faculty mentors if you are graduate school or faculty peers if you have graduated. Letter writers should know you well enough to address your teaching, research, collegiality, and motivation because letters that fail to address these key issues reflect negatively on the candidate (Ng, 1997). For example, if collegiality is not mentioned, search committees might infer that you are a jerk. Advisors expect requests for letters and know students well enough to write a fully supportive letter, but other faculty may say yes even though they are not familiar enough with a student's work to write the type of letter that will be beneficial. Give faculty members an opportunity to gracefully decline by asking if their experience working with you would allow them to write a detailed and positive recommendation letter (Vick et al., 2016). If they say no, it is a good thing because you have avoided a detrimentally banal letter.

Letters will be more beneficial if the writer can address your competency in relation to the specific requirements of a job (Darley & Zanna, 2004; Morgan & Landrum, 2012; Vick et al., 2016; Wells et al., 2013). Thus, you should select letter writers to match the position. Research-heavy institutions call for all of the letters writers to be from people who can vouch for your scholarly potential, and teaching-heavy institutions call for letter writers to all have knowledge of your teaching skills. Many positions will call for scholar–teachers, and selection of writers can be divided among faculty familiar with your research and faculty familiar with your teaching. For example, when I was applying to colleges that required teaching and scholarship (in that order), my graduate school letter writers included my advisor and a faculty coauthor who spoke mostly to scholarship, and I also got letters from the chair of undergraduate studies and a teaching mentor, both of whom had observed me in the classroom and spoke mostly to teaching.

Help your letter writers help you. Meet with them to share your application materials and summarize how you think their perspective on your work will be a valuable addition to your argument for being hired (Morgan & Landrum, 2012; Wells et al., 2013). If it is a research-focused or a teaching-focused position, make sure they know. You might also consider highlighting for letter writers your top positions so that they can take extra care in writing and sending those letters. Do not be afraid to tell letter writers about potential flaws in your application packages. Well-crafted letters can fill apparent weaknesses in a candidate's fit with a position. For example, search committees at teaching-focused institutions will be suspicious of candidates whose careers seemed to have emphasized research over teaching, but having letter writers explicitly state that the candidate wants a position at a teaching-focused college can assuage such fears. Or letter writers could explain a relative dearth of publications by emphasizing the applicant's goal to produce only high-quality, high-impact research.

Make the process easy for your letter-writers. Prepare a spreadsheet that contains an entry for each position (Huang-Pollock & Mikami, 2007). Include the due date, address for sending the letter, a link to the advertisement, and a link to the college's psychology department webpage. For mailed materials, check to see if letter writers want addressed and stamped envelopes. Preferences differ—some faculty cannot be bothered to copy an address, and others find it gauche to send letters in envelopes lacking the university insignia. Find out each letter writer's preference for dealing with letter requests and deadlines (Morgan & Landrum, 2012). Do they want a single batch of requests or multiple batches as new jobs appear and deadlines approach? Also, if an unexpected job opening with an imminent deadline pops up, how do they want to proceed? Finally, give them plenty of lead time to draft and send your letters; a month is the minimum standard of collegiality.

RULES FOR COMMUNICATING (OR NOT) WITH THE COLLEGE AND THE SEARCH COMMITTEE

We have all been there—you meet someone, become smitten, and must decide if and when to call or text. Do you make first contact or stay aloof? Both options risk putting off your new target of affection. This dilemma can also occur when you are smitten with a job. The lack of feedback after applying for faculty positions can be maddening. For some jobs, a rejection letter may be the first communication that you receive. Sometimes there will not even be an acknowledgment of having applied. Tossing your materials down a well would be equally rewarding. Thus, there is an understandable temptation to seek assurances by contacting the search committee; this can be an appropriate move, but there are some rules to follow.

Making contact to inquire about a job application should be approached strategically. As a rule, email is the preferred mode for all communications regarding an application (Brems et al., 1995; Schwebel & Karver, 2004).

Phone calls only go in one direction—from the college to the candidate—and only occur late in the search process. When emailing, be sure to contact the appropriate person. Although it is perfectly acceptable to check if an application file is complete (Vick et al., 2016), direct this question to the people doing the paperwork. Someone from human resources or a faculty secretary will probably be handing all of the application materials and creating files for each candidate.

Reaching out to members of the search committee to unofficially inquire about a position is risky. There is one school of thought that personal communications demonstrate interest in the position and will make a candidate stand out in the search committee members' memory when considering applications. If the communication is genuine, some search committee members may indeed appreciate this personal touch, but not all of them. Some will see a breach of protocol. During one search that I was a part of, a candidate hand-delivered application materials to a search committee member, and we were mortified. The lavender-colored paper did not help either. Bad form tends to cluster. If you know the person whom you are contacting, the riskiness of making personal inquiries goes down because of that established relationship. Similarly, if you have mentors with connections, they can reach out to suggest special consideration of your application (Vick et al., 2016). Overall, absence of communication from a candidate carries no risk, and any communication that does occur should consist of single, genuine emails directed to the correct person.

CONCLUSION

Going on the job market is a labor-intensive undertaking. The size of the task is affected by whether it is your first time on the market and how narrowly you are applying, but even applying for a single position requires dozens of steps spread across several months. Essentially, going on the market is like having a part-time job on top of all your other responsibilities. Just like any other important job, it requires organization and planning (for a checklist, see the book's companion website: http://pubs.apa.org/books/supp/boysen/). Although applying for jobs is stressful and time-consuming, the payoff comes when you get an invitation for an interview, which is the subject of the next chapter.

7

INTERVIEWING

As I write this, the college basketball season is drawing to a close, and excitement about the big tournament is starting to kick in. Part of what makes the NCAA basketball finals such a dramatic spectacle is that the tournament is a fresh slate, and each team—from perennial powerhouses to tourney first-timers—has a chance for the championship. Faculty interviews work the same way. Candidates from better schools with better curriculum vitae (CVs) may go in with an advantage, but any candidate who makes it to the interview stage has the basic qualifications needed to do the job, and each candidate might be the one to wow the search committee. During every faculty search, candidates who look great on paper disappoint in person, and candidates with middling CVs move up because of their dynamic interview style. It is still anyone's game.

The faculty interview game is quite complex. It can include meetings, interviews, presentations, meals, social events, and more spread across multiple days. Search committees determine the interview format, questions, and method of evaluation, so the only part of the process that candidates have control over is their own preparation. The purpose of this chapter is to

http://dx.doi.org/10.1037/0000152-008
Becoming a Psychology Professor: Your Guide to Landing the Right Academic Job,
by G. A. Boysen

outline how to prepare for the faculty interview process as it typically occurs for full-time faculty positions. The chapter breaks down into sections based on the standard components of the faculty interview, including the preliminary phone and video interviews and the follow-up interviews on campus. Each section contains a detailed description of what to expect and advice on how best to prepare and execute your preparations in person, including suggestions on how to nail the all-important job talk. In addition, this chapter acknowledges that the interview process goes both ways—they are evaluating you and you are evaluating them—and includes suggestions for questions to ask as interviews progress. Excellent candidates may end up with multiple job offers, and having asked the right questions during the interview will make the final decision easier.

PHONE AND VIDEO INTERVIEWS

My colleagues and I were in the second hour of a long series of phone interviews for an open faculty position. Everyone was draped over their chairs, finding it difficult to maintain cheery tones and fastidious note taking while asking the same questions over and over. Then a candidate woke us up. The answers were fresh, informed, and on point. Within a few minutes, we were laughing and having an engaging conversation; it no longer felt like an interview. A few minutes more and we had decided to invite the candidate to campus right away.

The magic of phone and video interviews is that candidates have an opportunity to turn themselves into real, dynamic individuals in the minds of search committee members. How can you come off as a person more valuable than the list of credentials on your CV? Prepare fastidiously (for a checklist, see this book's companion website: http://pubs.apa.org/books/supp/boysen/). Being prepared frees you up to act naturally, rather than wondering what is going on or scrambling for answers, and allows you to focus on developing rapport with the search committee. Prepared candidates know about both the format of the interview and the questions they are likely to face.

Interview Format

The first round of faculty interviews occurs via phone or video (Huang-Pollock & Mikami, 2007; Morgan & Landrum, 2012). These interviews last 15 to 30 minutes and are likely to include multiple members of the search committee, if not the whole group. The number of questions is dictated by interview length, but a rough estimate is that there will be one question for every 3 minutes of scheduled interview time. Interviews typically conclude with a chance for the candidate to ask a few questions.

Both phone and video interviews are now considered standard, and each format comes with unique advantages and disadvantages. Phone interviews provide an opportunity to set up and await the call in a command center of your choosing surrounded by outlined answers, notes on the position, lucky charms, pets, or anything else you find useful. The disadvantage of phone interviews is the stilted formalness of being put on speakerphone and having to answer questions with little to no social reinforcement from the people on the other end (Morgan & Landrum, 2012; Vick, Furlong, & Lurie, 2016). Even if the search committee loves every word coming out of your mouth, you may get nothing but dead air in return. Another disadvantage is that poor connections and the use of speakerphones can turn even brilliant orators into barely audible static monsters.

How can the impediments of phone interviews be overcome? Trite as it sounds, one way to build rapport is to smile your way through the interview (Vick et al., 2016). If you feel and look miserable, you will sound miserable, so be happy and enthused even if the search committee will only hear and not see it. My old trick was to watch funny clips from Conan O'Brien's show before each call so that I was relaxed and laughing just seconds before picking up the phone. In terms of the technological problem of being able to hear the committee, do not be afraid to ask them to repeat the questions or to repeat questions back to them to ensure that you heard them correctly. Also, accept that you will have to repeat an answer or two without being annoyed or thrown—your second attempt will be better anyway.

Some search committees have made the switch to video interviews. The good news if you have a video interview is that it allows a more natural social interaction because you can see the interviewers and their reactions to your answers. Just a simple nod will feel like an oasis of feedback after the nonverbal desert of phone interviews. However, technological difficulties can arise. Test your computer and Internet connection as best as you can before the interview. Also, ask the search chair beforehand what to do if there are technical problems and be flexible if they do occur; taking these precautions make you look good (Morgan & Landrum, 2012). Finally, be sure to clear your browser history because it will be visible to the search committee via the video conferencing software. Just kidding.

Although the committee will not be able to see what is on your computer, they will be able to see you and what is in your room. Hide your notes. Take down the Bob Marley poster. Let a neighbor walk your dog. Essentially, you have to treat a video interview like a face-to-face interview conducted in your home or office. The interview gives you the responsibilities of director in an extremely low-budget movie. You have to check the lighting, plan for eye lines (i.e., speak to the camera, not the screen), ensure that the camera angle is flattering, and call for quiet on the set (Vick et al., 2016). Arrange yourself and everything that can be seen or heard to give off a professional air.

Research and Preparation

Once applications are sent, you are officially on call. Invitations for the first round of interviews could come at any time. In one search I was part of, we were contacting applicants for on-campus interviews less than 3 weeks after the position was posted. Responding swiftly in setting up the interview reflects well on you as a candidate. Even if you have dozens of applications out, do not forget where you applied. Create a cheat sheet that lists colleges, names, and basic facts so that you can respond quickly if contacted by a college (Brems, Lampman, & Johnson, 1995; Huang-Pollock & Mikami, 2007). The wrong response when a search chair calls to set up an interview is "You are from where?"

Once the phone or video interview is set up, continue to research the college and the department (Darley & Zanna, 2004; Morgan & Landrum, 2012). You may have already done most of the required research as part of deciding where to apply and writing cover letters, but make sure that the information is fresh in your mind for the interview. What do you need to know? In terms of the institution, know the setting, mission, and basic history. In terms of teaching, be familiar with the student body, basic curricular requirements, and the names of courses you are likely to teach. For scholarship, know the research areas of faculty, typical publication patterns, and well-publicized research facilities and support. In general, be aware of anything the college or department clearly publicizes on their website or in their social media.

The next phase of preparation consists of anticipating interview questions and outlining answers. Notice the word choice there—*outlining*. Do not write out or memorize exact answers. Why not? Remember, interviews are the first chance job candidates have to come off as real, dynamic individuals, and relying on a script is no help here. By way of an analogy, with rare exceptions, I abhor old-timey movies, and the main reason is that the actors, rather than portraying normal human beings, seem like they are reading a script. Search committees do not like bad acting either, so you should create bullet-pointed answers to standard questions rather than writing out whole answers. By all means, memorize the bullet points, but not the verbatim answers. Even over the phone, it is clear when a candidate is giving a canned answer.

Another problem with memorizing complete answers is that they do not leave room for improvisation. There will be unanticipated questions, and you do not want to give robotic answers. Responding to unexpected questions with "Request does not compute" will not help your chances, but neither will barreling through a preset answer to a question the search committee did not ask. By preparing main points, you can pick and choose single points to create novel answers to questions that you did not specifically anticipate.

In terms of anticipating questions, Exhibit 7.1 outlines a sampling of general first-round interview questions. The list is by no means exhaustive, but your main points from these questions can easily be reshuffled into answers to similar questions. Create answers to your own questions based on the specific nature of your CV and the position. Some search committees will ask weird questions. I was once asked to name my three favorite psychologists, which seemed more appropriate for a first date than a job interview (Wegner, Freud, and Danzinger, by the way). The committee might be interested in your weird answers, or they want to know whether you can think on your feet. Do not worry too much about oddball questions, however, because basic questions about fit are most important.

Interviewing also requires the preparation of some questions for the search committee. It is standard for the final question of first-round interviews to be "What questions do you have for us?" As such, your questions are part of the interview too, and the search committee will use them to evaluate your fit with the position. You must have questions because a response of "None" sends a clear message that you are either not interested in the position or

---

EXHIBIT 7.1. First-Round Interview Questions

- Why do you want a position at this institution?
- What courses can you contribute to our curriculum, and what is your approach to them?
- What are your teaching methods, and what are specific examples of how you use them?
- What is your research about?
- What are your goals for future research, and how will you pursue them?
- How will you fund and conduct your research at this institution?
- The advertisement mentioned _____. What can you bring to our institution related to this? [Have an answer for all job requirements mentioned in the advertisement.]
- What are your questions for us?

have not bothered to prepare, and this is grounds for rejection (Boysen, Morton, & Nieves, in press). Having two to three questions for the committee is standard. However, do not be greedy with their time because they will be on a tight schedule with other interviews, and, again, the main point is for the committee to evaluate your questions, not for you to gather information.

At this stage in the interview process, the ideal question for candidates to ask will (a) include some detail that exhibits knowledge about the college and department, (b) demonstrate priorities that match the position, and (c) elicit positive answers. For example, a research-focused question might be "I noticed on your website that most of the faculty have continuous grant support, what does the program do to maintain such a record?" A teaching-focused question might be "I was able to see basic demographics of students on your website, but can you tell me about the typical students in your program?" Questions such as these will leave the committee with a positive feeling as the interview ends because everyone likes to brag about their program, and they will also have a sense that your interest in the position is informed and sincere.

There are three types of questions to avoid. One, do not ask questions that could be easily answered with a search of the college website (e.g., "Do you offer internships?" "Are there funds for travel?"). This sends the message that you did not do your research, which is a kiss of death (Boysen et al., in press). Two, do not ask questions indicative of a preference to work at a different type of institution. For example, do not ask about buying out of teaching at a baccalaureate college or about advising the psych club at a doctoral university because such questions suggest mismatching emphases on research and mentoring undergraduates, respectively. Three, do not ask questions that are only relevant after you have a job offer (e.g., "What is the starting pay?" "Can I apply for tenure early?"). Impudence kills candidacies.

The first round of interviews is like the initial meeting for a drink or coffee that people have to evaluate potential mates before committing to a full date. The first interaction is not as important as the full date, but it is used to screen out people who are a bad match. In other words, the only way to get to the real date, or an on-campus interview in this case, is to excel during that first meeting.

THE ON-CAMPUS INTERVIEW

What is an on-campus interview like? Here is a blow-by-blow example of one of my more memorable ones. The search chair picked me up at the airport in the late afternoon and took me to an apartment on campus that

I could not leave because I did not have a key to get back into the building. After some downtime, I went to dinner at an upscale restaurant with *one* member of the department. On this "interview date" I had to do most of the conversational work because my companion was even less adept at small talk than me. The interview-day itinerary started at 7:45 a.m. the next morning, and my escort to breakfast inexplicably showed up at 7:15—I was lucky to be dressed. Breakfast was a merciful "three-way date" with two faculty members. The day itself was a blur: I gave a research presentation to faculty, I gave a teaching demonstration to students, I met three administrators, I had interviews and open times with faculty, and I got no breaks whatsoever. On the way to another fancy dinner, I received a tour of the community and, for some reason, the house of the person driving me. It was a nice house. Dinner ended at 9 p.m., and I was alone for the first time that day by 9:30. All told, it was almost 15 straight hours of interviewing.

Although that is a busy day for anyone, whether you see it as a punishing bore, invigorating adventure, or anxiety-riddled nightmare is a product of your personality and professional experiences. Introverts, such as myself, will find it exhausting to meet and be relatively engaging with dozens of new people in one day, but extroverts may wish that every day could be as interpersonally exciting as a job interview. Likewise, people with little classroom experience may find teaching demonstrations intimidating, but if, like me, you deliver a lesson after honing it for several semesters in actual classes, you can relax and focus on trying to impart some knowledge. Personality and experience aside, interviews are stressful, but knowing what to expect and preparing helps (for a checklist, see the book's companion website: http://pubs.apa.org/books/supp/boysen/).

Format and Logistics

At 4-year colleges and universities, the on-campus interview is a 1- or 2-day event. It includes meetings with faculty, administrators, and students, some of which may be formal interviews. Less formally, there will be social events such as meals and receptions. Finally, there is the job talk; depending on the institution, job talks consist of a research presentation, a teaching presentation, or both. Every aspect of interviews will be planned and paid for by the institution (travel to the interview sometimes excluded). You just have to show up and perform.

Community college interviews are different (Franz, Manbur, & Neufeld, 2014; Jenkins, 2018; Twombly, 2005). Some of the same events occur, but they are condensed into a few hours rather than a sprawling, multiday affair. In addition, the job talk will be a teaching demonstration, and it too will be condensed to a single, short lesson rather than a full class period. Because community colleges tend to recruit locally, travel to the interview will be your responsibility.

Notification about your selection for an on-campus interview is likely to come in the form of an email from the search committee chair. Once the chair sends that email, the interview process has officially begun. Your promptness, enthusiasm, communication style, and flexibility are all being evaluated while setting up the particulars of the interview; any failings can lead to rejection even at this early stage (Boysen et al., in press). You can convey enthusiasm and independence by immediately accepting the first interview date (Huang-Pollock & Mikami, 2007). You read that correctly—date in the singular. The logistics of organizing entire days of events for multiple candidates can prevent the committee from extending a choice of interview dates, and, aside from having another interview already scheduled, the expectation is that you accept what is offered. Trust me, bailing on that class or research meeting will seem paltry once you land a job.

After the interview is scheduled, the research and planning process begins. Politely ask the chair who is involved in the search process and the logistics of any presentations you will need to make during the interview (Darley & Zanna, 2004). Do some reconnaissance on every person you will meet during the interview so that you know his or her background and role at the university. Search committees will expect you to know more about the position than you did during the phone interview. So, continue to explore information about the college online so that you appear knowledgeable during the interview and to identify questions and concerns about potential employer. Finally, start perfecting every nuance of that job talk.

Nailing the Job Talk

How important is the job talk? I have been on search committees that hired no one because the all of the candidates' job talks were lackluster—not terrible, they did not start a fire or punch a dean, just lackluster. Conversely, I have seen job talks that were so spectacular as to overshadow otherwise glaring flaws in the candidates' professional potential. Think about these two extremes for moment. Job talks are so influential that they can prevent a search committee from hiring otherwise qualified candidates or convince them to hire flawed candidates.

Two variations of the job talk exist: the research talk and the teaching presentation. *Research talks* consist of oral presentations of a candidate's program of research, typically focusing on the results of specific studies. Surveys of faculty indicate that research talks are required at 86% of doctoral universities, 63% of master's universities, and 51% of baccalaureate colleges (Boysen, Jones, Kaltwasser, & Thompson, 2018). In contrast, *teaching demonstrations* consist of instructing a sample class, and they are required at 21% of doctoral universities, 47% of master's universities, and 59% of baccalaureate colleges (Boysen et al., 2018). A significant number of baccalaureate colleges (33%) and master's universities (22%) require both types of talks.

Surveys also indicate that, other than basic fit with the position, the job talk is one of the most important factors in determining who gets hired (Benson & Buskist, 2005; Ng, 1997; Sheehan et al., 1998). Thus, candidates must "prepare for, practice, and 'nail' the job talk and any undergraduate classroom presentation during the interview"(Benson & Buskist, 2005, p. 48). This is great advice, but nailing a job talk requires consideration of format and institution type.

The Research Talk

The standard format for a research talk is an oral presentation accompanied by PowerPoint slides. Talks are 40 to 50 minutes with additional time for questions (Darley & Zanna, 2004; Huang-Pollock & Mikami, 2007; Iacono, 1981; Wells, Schofield, Clerkin, & Sheets, 2013). The typical setting is an open meeting attended mostly by faculty at master's universities and baccalaureate colleges but by a mixed audience of faculty and students at doctoral universities (Boysen et al., 2018). These are only generalities, however, so find out as many details as possible before the interview so that you can prepare accordingly (Morgan & Landrum, 2012). It is essential to aim your research talk for the right audience.

Experts generally agree on the basic structure job candidates should follow in a research talk (Darley & Zanna, 2004; Huang-Pollock & Mikami, 2007; Morgan & Landrum, 2012). A 50-minute talk will contain the following sections, each one of roughly equal length:

- introduction and background,
- method,
- results,
- discussion and summary, and
- future research plans.

Presenting multiple studies is a good way to demonstrate your record as a programmatic researcher (Darley & Zanna, 2004; Wells et al., 2013), and faculty will be closely evaluating this trait during the talk (Boysen et al., 2018). However, plowing through a half-dozen studies may not be to your advantage because you will not be able to communicate that amount of material clearly to a mixed audience of people unfamiliar with your research (Boysen et al., 2018; Darley & Zanna, 2004; Huang-Pollock & Mikami, 2007; Wells et al., 2013). You are being evaluated on both research skills and public speaking skills.

After the presentation comes the questions, and some consider the Q and A performance to be more important than the prepared content. Respect the time set aside for questions even if it means skipping over some details during your presentation. Your ability to respond to questions in a meaningful, nondefensive, and respectful manner is part of what defines a successful research talk (Boysen et al., 2018, in press). Answering questions well is a skill that must be planned for and practiced just like any other aspect of a job talk.

There are several strategies for answering questions during a job talk. Legitimate and direct questions deserve legitimate and direct answers, even if they require the admission of a research limitation. Any limitation you acknowledge can be framed as a topic for "future research." Another type of question asked at every research talk ever given is some variation of "The concept of X seems to have direct implications on your work; how did you account for it?" which roughly translates into "I research concept X and want to talk about it in front of all these people." In response to such off-topic questions, say, "Thank you, that's a great question!" and then give an answer that emphasizes the strengths of your research program (Kelsky, 2015). You can also reframe off-topic questions as topics for future research. If someone is really out of control, mistaking your job talk for a senate filibuster or the Spanish Inquisition, you can say, "I would love to talk more after the presentation" and move to the next person with a question (Huang-Pollock & Mikami, 2007). Do not be scared or defensive; everyone knows that person is a jerk, and handling the situation democratically makes you look like a pro.

Although good research and public speaking skills are valued at all types of institutions, some variations in research talks are required to match to research- and teaching-focused institutions. Faculty at doctoral universities will focus heavily on evidence of programmatic research (Boysen et al., 2018), so presenting a single study, unrelated studies, or vague plans for future studies is not an option. Doctoral faculty also value independence from research mentors; they will be looking for your ability to direct your own work and mentor graduate students. To convey independence, you should start replacing "we" with "I" when talking about your research, and some of what you present should truly be your research, not follow-ups on the work of others. Finally, keep in mind that the research talk also serves as a demonstration of teaching ability (Boysen et al., 2018; Buddie, 2014; Meizlish & Kaplan, 2008; Sternberg, 2017). At research-focused institutions, it may be the most teaching-related thing that you do, so be polished and interesting enough that audience members can imagine students wanting to take a class with you.

At teaching-focused institutions, faculty will evaluate the candidate's ability to conduct research that is consistent with the institution's mission (Boysen et al., 2018). Because the mission at these colleges revolves around undergraduate education, the research talk should emphasize opportunities for undergraduate involvement. Furthermore, faculty will be closely evaluating your potential as a teacher, so it is essential to engage the audience, be responsive to questions, and make even the most complex research concepts accessible to undergraduates.

The Teaching Demonstration

Teaching demonstrations are like tryouts for a sports team: They are an opportunity to demonstrate, albeit in a highly artificial setting, the skills needed to be successful in a real-world scenario. At 4-year colleges, the audience will be mix of students and faculty, and it will likely consist of a "guest lecture" in a standing course (Boysen et al., 2018). This translates into a 40- to 50-minute lesson. On what? That is a good question that may or may not have a predetermined answer. At the extremes, the search committee may grant you total freedom to select your best material, or you may be asked to teach the topic that is already scheduled to be covered on the day of class.

At community colleges, there will be a "micro-teaching" demonstration. These demonstrations consist of 15- to 20-minute lessons presented to faculty on a specific topic from general psychology (Ewing, 2014; Franz et al., 2014; Twombly, 2005). Treat this presentation as a single, short lesson from a larger class, and treat the faculty just as you would students in that class (Jenkins, 2004b, 2018). Performance expectations are the same as a full teaching demonstration, you just have less time to impress.

No matter the format or topic, you must approach the teaching demonstration as opportunity to show off your mastery of pedagogical skills. Of course, one way to blow a teaching demonstration is to not know what you are talking about—accuracy is essential—but surveys of faculty indicate that getting the audience interested, interacting with them, and answering their questions are key to successful teaching demonstrations (Boysen et al., 2018). To be perfectly clear, being engaging is essential regardless of teaching method. Opinions differ on what counts as student engagement. Some would accept a few dynamic examples or YouTube videos during 50 minutes of lecture as engagement. Others view 50-minutes of lecture as inherently unengaging; they would only count active learning—discussion, application, problem-solving—as properly engaging.

If you use active learning in your teaching, then incorporate it into your teaching demonstration. Some graduate advisors mistakenly claim that teaching demonstrations must be lectures because, after all, it is the teacher is who is being evaluated. This is bad advice. Even in the most cavernous, impersonal lecture hall imaginable, there are ways to engage students by having them actively think about or work with the material; missing these opportunities is failure of pedagogy, and search committees at schools that value good teaching will take notice. Even something as simple as "pair up and share your answers to this question" can save an otherwise ponderous lecture-based teaching demonstration.

Going beyond just being engaging, teaching demonstrations are also opportunities to demonstrate consistency with model teaching characteristics (Richmond, Boysen, & Gurung, 2016; Society for the Teaching of Psychology, 2013). Start the lesson by outlining the learning objectives. Be sure that the objectives are written as measurable outcomes and that they can actually be achieved during one lesson. Implement some pedagogical techniques known to increase learning such as self-generation of answers, deep processing, testing knowledge, or collaboration. Then conduct a formative assessment of student learning. Keep it simple—I am not arguing for a pop quiz here—and have students write down and report one of their unanswered questions or have them answer a multiple-choice question posted on the screen. Further demonstrate the ability to use active learning by having them discuss the results. End well. Go back to the learning objectives, offer a summary, and preview what you would be covering next if it were a regular course.

Meetings! Meetings! Meetings!

No other aspect of the on-campus interview process contributes more to its whirlwind atmosphere than the long string of meetings with, perhaps, dozens of people whom you may or may not see again. Although some of the people you meet may seem far removed from your immediate goals— during one interview I was driven to a far-off, nondescript annex that served as the human resources office and fleetingly wondered how many CIA renditions began with a similar trip to a secondary location—keep in mind that you are always on a job interview. Each person you meet provides a valuable perspective on what life is like at the college, and everyone you interact with can provide candidacy-ending feedback to the search committee about what it would be like to have you as a colleague (Boysen et al., in press). Once, after meeting a very, very famous psychologist, the one anecdote a colleague shared about the experience was that the person was rude to a waiter. Avoid all such anecdotes. Do not be a jerk. Be professional, engaged, polite, and easygoing with every person you interact with during a campus interview.

Meetings With Faculty

Most meetings during an on-campus interview will involve faculty. The three basic variations of these meetings are informal discussions, formal interviews, and open sessions. Some faculty will just chat informally in an effort to form an impression of candidates. Other faculty, most likely members of the search committee, will want candidates to answer specific questions in classic job-interview style; this may happen one-on-one or with multiple members of the committee. Finally, in larger departments, candidates may be presented to all comers during an open session where faculty come and go as their schedules allow. Because community college interviews are condensed, there may be just one meeting with all of the faculty in which they ask standardized questions (Franz et al., 2014).

No matter the format, meetings with faculty are one of the main factors that go into the final decision of who to hire (Sheehan et al., 1998). Whether it is obvious or not, faculty at every meeting will be evaluating your qualifications, fit with the department, and collegiality. So, the main goals during these meetings are to (a) emphasize your main arguments for fit with the department and (b) maintain a positive and engaging demeanor (Huang-Pollock & Mikami, 2007; Sternberg, 2017; Vick et al., 2016). Unfortunately, faculty meetings can be subjective and political. Rubbing just one faculty member the wrong way can end a candidacy because people believe, with some merit, that anyone who cannot get through an interview without putting people off would be a nightmare if permanently installed in the department.

Several interview strategies can increase the chances you will convey your key message of competence and make a positive personal impression. One strategy for ensuring consistency in your message is to practice answering standard on-campus interview questions, which are outlined later in the chapter. There is no need to memorize most of the answers, but have main points in mind. However, because you are likely to encounter the same questions about your educational background, teaching, research, and service interests over and over, you can script out 1-minute elevator speeches on these topics.

Another strategy is to conduct research on all the faculty you will be meeting with during the interview (Wells et al., 2013). Prepare notes on each faculty member in relation to his or her educational history, specialty area, teaching, research, and commonalities or interests that you share. Doing background research provides a sense of what each faculty member values and what you are likely to talk about when you meet. Even the smallest of commonalities can smooth over the initial awkwardness of the interview. One of the most enjoyable interviews I ever had was largely based on the totally irrelevant fact that the search chair and I shared a love for Bob Dylan. I have a colleague who is a master at using commonalities to strengthen her professional network. Her most spectacular example is the professional friendship she started after spotting a woman at a conference wearing the same glasses, introducing herself, and eventually saying, "Hey, I think we have the same glasses!" Small connections can make a big interpersonal difference.

One of the best strategies for a successful interview is to get the people you are interviewing to talk about everyone's favorite topic: themselves. Ask lots of questions about people's educational background and their work. If the person who is supposed to be doing the interviewing spends most of the time talking about things they love, then they will enjoy meeting you, even if they do not leave with much information about you.

Meetings With Administrators

In addition to faculty, the on-campus interview often includes meetings with three administrators: the department chair, a dean or provost, and a human resources representative. Meetings with administrators are important but less impactful on the final hiring decision than other factors (Sheehan, McDevitt, & Ross, 1998). These meetings focus on factual information about the position, such as contractual responsibilities, performance expectations, and benefits (Darley & Zanna, 2004; Huang-Pollock & Mikami, 2007; Iacono, 1981). The chair and the dean/provost meetings may take the format of a traditional interview, but the human resources meeting will consist of a recitation of facts related to dependents, copays, retirement funds, withholdings, pretax contributions, and a bunch of other stuff you stayed in college for a decade to avoid thinking about.

The department chair is the most important administrator interview for several reasons. Because he or she is part of the department, the chair will be able to communicate directly with the search committee about your suitability, and the chair's opinion will have more weight than average because he or she is respected and influential enough to have received an administrative appointment. In addition, chairs are often responsible for decisions such as class scheduling, distribution of funds, and service assignments, so he or she will be able to answer questions about the functioning of the department.

On-campus interviews will also include a meeting with the dean or provost. People with the title of dean are in charge of academic affairs, sort of like the chair of chairs, and people with the title of provost are a sort of vice president that has the official responsibility of hiring and firing faculty. These meetings are largely about money and college policy (Kelsky, 2015). As the person in charge of academic budgets, the administrator will be trying to figure out how much it would cost to hire you based on potential salary, start-up costs, grants that you might bring in, and maintenance of your research program. In terms of college policy, the administrator will talk with you about the contractual requirements of the job and the tenure process; the goal of this talk is to assess whether you can meet the institution's standards. These are strange meetings because the dean or provost has the power to reject the search committee's recommendation for a hire, but there is no way to determine what, if any, influence they will exert. Regardless of their eventual influence, your goal should be to emphasize your ability to succeed in the position and to do so at relatively little cost.

Meetings With Students

Most interviews will include a meeting with students, and they are especially common at baccalaureate colleges (Meizlish & Kaplan, 2008). There is no standard format for these meetings, but they are likely to be informal and include several students; lunch at the cafeteria is a popular option. The meetings occur outside of regular class time, but they are a method for evaluating candidates' teaching ability. The search committee wants to determine if you can engage with students and if they feel comfortable with you.

On a day-to-day basis, faculty have more contact with students than any other group of people at their college, so the culture and quality of students is a significant factor in work satisfaction. As such, even if a college does not schedule an official meeting with students, ask if you can meet some of them (Vick et al., 2016). Requesting the meeting demonstrates a positive investment in students, and the actual meeting provides an opportunity for you to find out information that might otherwise be obscured. What are the students like? Would you like to work with them? Do they complain?

Are they embroiled in departmental politics? Keep in mind that the department will try to ensure that you meet its best students, so any negativity is omen of ill health in the department or college (Iacono, 1981).

A job candidate's prime directive during these meetings is to show interest in the students and their perspectives. The worst possible outcome is that students go back to the faculty and report that you were haughty or disinterested. A secondary goal is to convince the students that your teaching and research focuses on really, really interesting stuff that they will want to be involved with. If the students leave thinking you are nice person and someone they would like to learn from, you have succeeded.

Meals and Social Events

Interviews at 4-year institutions will include meals and, perhaps, a social event such as a reception or party. Treat these events like they are your birthday party; no, you should not ask for presents or to be serenaded with annoying songs, but you do have to stay for the whole event and show humble appreciation for people's generosity and time (Darley & Zanna, 2004). Even though you are the titular center of these gatherings, be conversational, ask questions, and show interest in what people have to say (Vick et al., 2016).

Depending on the culture of the institution, meals and social events may be casual, requiring no more social grace than a trip to the campus cafeteria, or they may be formal functions that test candidates' ability to fit into society. To job candidates, these events can seem like series of etiquette traps ready to spring at any moment. Table 7.1 lists some common concerns and ways to deal with them.

ON-CAMPUS INTERVIEW QUESTIONS
YOU SHOULD BE PREPARED TO ANSWER

Answering questions about qualifications and interest in a position are fundamental parts of the job-interview process. Unlike phone interviews, questions during on-campus interviews will arise more organically, and there will be sufficient time to offer in-depth answers. As such, on-campus interviews require more than 1-minute elevator speeches; answers should provide details to back up broad arguments for fit with the position. For example, on the phone, the questions might be "What is your research about?" and "Can you teach statistics?" but on campus, the questions would be "How does the program of research you propose fit with other faculty in the department?" and "How would you approach the instruction of statistics in our curriculum?" At this point, the interview is about selecting the person

TABLE 7.1. Interview-Based Social Traps and Escape Maneuvers

Social trap	Ways to escape
To drink or not to drink.	Follow the lead of the people at the event to determine whether drinking is acceptable and what you can order without seeming like an alcoholic (e.g., double anything) or a rube (e.g., Goldschläger). Do not drink alone.
How much to drink.	Do not drink more than others. Do not get buzzed.
What to order at a restaurant.	Order safe food that is not messy and not likely to poison you. Do not order anything with a price that will make you stand out from the group.
How to act at a fancy restaurant.	Watch what the people around you are doing and copy them. Better yet, before the interview, treat your most cultured mentor to the fanciest dinner you can afford and have them walk you through the basics (e.g., forks, types of wine, napkin placement).
Making small talk.	Prepare topics of conversation. Prepare questions that will get people talking about themselves. Practice talking to people.
What to wear or not wear.	Wear business attire that you will be comfortable in all day. Try to be at or one notch above everyone else in terms of formality. Clothing and accessories should not distract you or the people around you.
I have to go to the bathroom!	Say, "Please excuse me, I need a brief break, can you point me to a restroom?" and use the restroom.

who will actually be following through with his or her answers, and the answers have real implications for the department.

Interview questions tend to be about the general topics of research, teaching, and contributions to the program. Specifically, questions will relate to plans for publication, your specialty area, courses you can teach, teaching methods, what you can contribute to the department and college, and your commitment to being a professor at the college (Kelsky, 2015). However, the form these questions take will vary based on institution. Tables 7.2, 7.3, and 7.4 outline some sample questions you should be prepared to answer when interviewing at different types of institutions.

There is another class of questions that job candidates need to be prepared for: illegal ones. Interviewers are legally prohibited from asking about age, race, gender, country of origin, religion, family status, or disability. I was once involved in a search where two out of three final candidates were stupendously pregnant—a fact the search committee assiduously ignored as if a hypnotist had implanted the suggestion that we could no longer perceive people's torsos. Not everyone is so disciplined, however, and illegal questions come up, directly or indirectly, all the time (Huang-Pollock & Mikami, 2007;

TABLE 7.2. On-Campus Interview Questions About Research

College type	Interview questions
	General topic: What is your specialty area?
Research-focused	• How do you fill our research needs?
	• How does your research fit in with the current faculty, and what collaborations might occur?
	• How will you train graduate students in a valuable research area?
Teaching-focused	• What content areas can you fill in our department?
	• What courses can you teach in our curriculum?
Community college	• What can you teach?
	General topic: What are your research plans?
Research-focused	• What systematic program of research do you have planned?
	• How will you form an independent research program?
	• How will you fund your research?
	• How will you conduct your research given local resources and facilities?
	• Where do you plan to publish your work?
	• What opportunities can you provide for graduate students?
Teaching-focused	• How will you do your research here?
	• How will you continue to be active in your field?
	• How will you provide opportunities for undergraduates?
	• How will you balance research with teaching?
Community college	• How do you stay up-to-date in the field?

Kelsky, 2015; Vick et al., 2016). These topics are forbidden to prevent discrimination in hiring, but they may emerge as normal topics of conversation or because people are interested and simply do not know any better. During my job interviews, people asked if I was married and if I had any kids; they were being friendly, albeit daft, so I simply answered.

As a young, White, heterosexual man from Minnesota, I had the privilege of simply answering illegal questions without a second thought because I had the "right" answers. Illegal questions are more precarious for the groups they are designed to protect. Job candidates face a catch-22 with illegal questions: Answer and risk discrimination, or do not answer and risk being perceived as difficult. Experts offer some possible strategies in responding (Kelsky, 2015; Vick et al., 2016). One option is to deflect. That is, ignore the original question, and say something positive about your qualifications or commitment to the position. Or answer the question by addressing the concerns that led to it being asked: "I find that my age/gender/family/nationality provide me with the resources I need to be successful in my work. I think the clearest sign of success is . . . ." Another approach is to answer the question as directly as possible but signal the end of the discussion by offering no

TABLE 7.3. On-Campus Interview Questions About Teaching

College type	Interview questions
	General topic: What courses do you teach?
Research-focused	• What courses would you like to teach? • What unique contributions can you make to our curriculum? • How would you approach mentorship of graduate students?
Teaching-focused	• How do you fit a gap in our course coverage? • What experiences do you have that show your committed to teaching undergraduates? • What service courses would you like to teach (e.g., general education, introductory psychology)? • How can you contribute to our specialized curriculum? • Are you willing to step up if we need a course covered?
Community college	• What courses in our curriculum can you teach? • What is your preparation to teach a wide variety of courses? • How do you ensure that all students learn in your courses?
	General topic: What are your teaching methods?
Research-focused	• What is your teaching philosophy? • How have you prepared to start teaching? • How you would approach your courses here?
Teaching-focused	• What is your teaching philosophy? • How has your experience prepared you to teach? • How do you engage students? • How do you incorporate evidence-based teaching methods? • How do you teach the liberal arts skills? • How would you teach the type of students that we have here? • What would be your approach to advising?
Community college	• What is your teaching philosophy? • How have you prepared to teach open-enrollment courses? • How would you teach the type of students that we have here? • What is your approach to mentoring students?

elaboration: "Yes, I am married." Finally, the most confrontational approach is to bring attention to question's irrelevance: "Is my marital status related to the job requirements?" No matter the approach taken, maintain a calm, professional demeanor.

QUESTIONS TO ASK DURING THE ON-CAMPUS INTERVIEW

Interviews go both ways; you can and should have questions prepared to ask during your on-campus interviews. Imagine being on a blind date with a person who declined to ask you any questions when given the opportunity—it is a clear sign of disinterest. People you meet with on an interview will ask if you have questions, and a response of "No" is not the right answer, even if

TABLE 7.4. On-Campus Interview Questions About Contribution and Commitment

College type	Interview questions
General topic: What can you contribute to the department and college?	
Research focused	• How can you improve our research reputation? • What special expertise can you bring here?
Teaching focused	• What can you contribute to our curriculum? • How will your teaching fit into our department? • How can undergraduates benefit from your expertise or scholarship? • What service are you interested in doing?
Community college	• What can you contribute to our curriculum? • How will you ensure teaching success in an open-enrollment setting? • What service are you interested in doing?
General topic: Why do you want to be at this college?	
Research focused	• How is your research going to fit in here? • How committed are you to publishing and finding funding?
Teaching focused	• How committed are you to teaching? • How committed are you to working with our type of students? • How do you see yourself fitting in to the unique mission (e.g., religious, liberal arts) of the college?
Community college	• How committed are you committed to teaching? • How committed are you to teaching students of diverse backgrounds and abilities? • How do you see yourself fitting into the community college mission?

it is true. Asking questions is expected, and failure to do so is a kiss of death (Boysen et al., in press). Select questions carefully, however.

There are many sources with lists of questions to ask when interviewing for psychology faculty positions (Darley & Zanna, 2004; Horner, Pape, & O'Connor, 2001; Morgan & Landrum, 2012; Wells et al., 2013). These lists are useful, but remember that questions are part of the larger message that you are trying to send about your strengths as a candidate. Only ask questions that are consistent with the argument you have been making for fit with the position ever since you wrote your cover letter. Interviewers want you to ask questions because they are an important way to assess your priorities and fit (Kelsky, 2015). For example, "What is the procedure for requesting start-up costs?" is a perfectly legitimate question at a doctoral university, but it could end a job candidacy if asked at a community college.

At doctoral universities, the main message to convey is "I will be a productive researcher." Examples of question topics that are consistent with this message include the following: research support, research performance expectations, grants, the grants office, subject pool availability, laboratory space, release time for research, advising graduate students, and graduate versus undergraduate teaching assignments.

For master's universities, the main message is: "I will be an active researcher and a dedicated teacher," perhaps in that order but maybe the reverse. Examples of topics that are consistent with this message include the following: research support, research expectations, graduate versus under-graduate teaching assignments, graduate and undergraduate inclusion in research, teaching performance expectations, and academic advising.

At baccalaureate colleges, the main message is: "I am dedicated to student-centered undergraduate education." Examples of topics that are consistent with this message include the following: teaching load, oppor-tunities to teach special courses (e.g., honors, general education), student characteristics, inclusion of undergraduates in research, teaching performance expectations, the teaching center, academic advising, and advising student organizations.

Finally, at community colleges, the main message is: "I am dedicated to teaching diverse students and helping them to develop and succeed aca-demically." Examples of topics that are consistent with this message include the following: teaching load, student characteristics, teaching performance expectations, academic advising, advising student organizations, and opportunities for student mentorship in and out of the classroom.

In addition to questions that reinforce your fit with the position, there are some questions that are equally valid at all types of institutions. These are questions about generic quality of academic life, such as:

- How clear and fair have you found the tenure/promotion/reappointment process to be?
- How do the faculty get along professionally and socially?
- How do faculty members from diverse backgrounds fit in here?
- What is the relationship between faculty and administration?
- What is it like to live in this area in terms of costs and culture?
- What are the best and worst aspects of working here?
- What will this institution be like in 5 to 10 years?

By asking different people these same questions, you start to identify themes that make the position look attractive or unattractive.

A primary goal of interviews is to make a good impression, but you should be assessing whether they are making a good impression on you as well (Huang-Pollock & Mikami, 2007; Sternberg, 2017; Vick et al., 2016).

You should be asking yourself, "Would I accept a job offer from this college?" At one of my job interviews, a faculty member sniggered asking, "Have you had your interview with the president yet? Just wait until you see the couch." True enough, the president and vice president of the university sat across from me in tall, wingback chairs while I squatted submissively on a brown, leather couch so low that I can only assume that the legs were sawed off during some long-forgotten mahogany shortage. For an hour or so, the administrators quizzed me on the finer points of my CV, occasionally sharing jokes I was not privy to, leading me to wonder, "Am I being hazed?" The interview felt like satire, and that was an omen that affected my answer to the question "Would I accept a job offer from this college?"

8 JOB OFFERS AND NEGOTIATIONS

Getting "the call" is a career-highlight moment. Mine came from the provost just as my wife and I were pulling into our driveway, coming home from the jobs we would be leaving in a few months. "Should I answer it?" I asked. "Yes!" my wife yelled, just as anxious as I was to hear the final news. A minute later, I had a job offer.

Dealing with offers and negotiations are an inevitable part of becoming a psychology professor, and preparing for the moment when you get the call is essential. The job hunt is grueling and intensely competitive; thus, it is tempting to shout, "I accept!" as soon as you hear "congratulations." This is not a marriage proposal, however, and immediate acceptance is neither expected nor encouraged, although throwing in an appreciative "I love you" would be a novel, if unorthodox, negotiation tactic.

No matter how hard it is to wait after getting an offer, the only correct way to end that initial phone call is "Thank you, I am very excited about the position, and I will need some time to consider the offer further." Also, no matter how uncomfortable it is to demand better terms, the only correct response to an initial offer is "I have considered your initial offer, it is very

http://dx.doi.org/10.1037/0000152-009
Becoming a Psychology Professor: Your Guide to Landing the Right Academic Job,
by G. A. Boysen

attractive, but I would like to negotiate some of the terms." Both of these strategies—waiting and negotiating—are standard practice and will benefit your final hiring package if used correctly. The purpose of this chapter is to provide strategies for dealing with offers so that you end up with a job that fits your needs, the resources to be successful at the job, and benefits commensurate to your value as a new member of the professorial ranks.

THE JOB OFFER TIMELINE

One of the maddening aspects of interviewing for a position is the subsequent waiting period. After an on-campus interview, final word on a position could take anywhere from days to months (Horner, Pape, & O'Connor, 2001; Schwebel & Karver, 2004). Two factors influence the length of the wait. The first factor is where a candidate is in the order of on-campus interviews. For the first candidate to interview for a position, there might automatically be 3 weeks or more of waiting because there are more candidates to interview, the search committee has to meet to make a decision, and the decision needs to be approved by at least one level of administration.

The second factor that determines wait time for an offer is whether a candidate is the first choice for the hire. Not being the top choice is a disheartening prospect to consider, but it happens. When an offer goes out to another candidate, that person may take some time to make a final decision, and then there may be a delay in notifying the other candidates as paperwork and background checks undergo final clearance. If that first choice accepts another offer or lied about their multiple felony convictions, then the offer will go out to the second choice after what could be weeks of delay.

Communication is key during what can be a protracted wait for final notification about a position. At the end of an on-campus interview, it is perfectly acceptable to ask the search chair to notify you if there is any change in the status of the job. If the chair is organized and merciful, he or she will inform candidates who interviewed on campus once an offer has been accepted. Candidates should likewise inform search chairs about any changes in their status, especially when they have other offers. The prospect of losing a desirable candidate could speed up the process, leading to a second offer, which is advantageous for the candidate (Darley & Zanna, 2004; Iacono, 1981; Kelsky, 2015). Being able to use one college's offer to sweeten the offer from another college is the ideal position to be in as a job candidate.

It may take weeks or months to learn about the final status of a position after an on-campus interview, but that does not mean you have an equal amount of time to make a decision once you have received a job offer. Think about the timeline from the search committee's perspective. Every day the committee waits for their first choice to make a decision, the chances of losing their second and third choices goes up. So once the offer is made, candidates will be under pressure to come to a decision as quickly as possible (Vick, Furlong, & Lurie, 2016). Experts suggest that candidates have about 2 weeks to make a decision (Darley & Zanna, 2004; Huang-Pollock & Mikami, 2007). However, deadlines can vary dramatically, and there will be pressure to commit quickly. Overall, you must stop and take the time to fully consider an offer once you receive it, but your time for deliberation is finite.

FINAL QUESTIONS TO ASK YOURSELF BEFORE ACCEPTING AN OFFER

By the time an official job offer is extended, you will have been thinking about the college and the position for months. Nonetheless, there are still some questions to ask yourself before starting the process of negotiation and acceptance. Here are some important final questions to consider.

Is it *really* a good fit? It is possible that you have been stretching the truth about your interests or expertise to get a job offer. Now, you have to decide if the job will still be rewarding and exciting in 5, 10, or 15 years. You also need to consider whether you can get tenure, or otherwise be successful, without burning yourself out. The requirements for success in academia can be inhumane, but they are self-inflicted.

Will taking the job help my career? Even if we are all psychology professors, where we work affords a certain level of status that is largely based on the scope of college's reputation and its emphasis on research. Moving down in status is easier than moving up, so experts recommend shooting for the highest status job possible when starting out (Vick et al., 2016). Not everyone starts out at their dream job. Many faculty members work up to a better position by using their first position to bolster their credentials. Avoid positions or jobs that will be a dead-end for your career aspirations.

Is the institution in transition? Colleges are often rising or falling, and those that fall take faculty with them. Chances are that nobody was padlocking the doors as you walked away from your interview, but enrollment patterns, endowments, hiring patterns, and accreditation body warnings can foretell the types of transitions that haunt the nightmares of academics. Institutions may also be in transition because they are striving for more academic prestige (O'Meara, 2007). Signs of this type of change include increased selectivity, reduced teaching load, increased demands for research, increased rigor, and adding graduate programs. If you like the direction of these changes, then the transition is a good thing, but taking a position at a college that is actively seeking increased prestige could lead to a change in the expectations for tenure and promotion after you have already started.

Will you and your family be happy in the community? Jobs are scarce and should be turned down with only the most serious of consideration, but family relationships are a major predictor of life satisfaction and health (Myers, 1999). If your partner or family is going to be miserable because of where you have forced them to move, then you will suffer as well.

Does the institution follow through with stated values about diversity? Every institution claims to value diversity, but some attract diverse faculty, staff, and students while others fail. Did your experience on campus match the institution's professed values related to diversity? Is diversity reflected across all aspects of the institution? Is there support for diverse students and faculty? Answers to these types of questions predict what you can expect on campus in the long term.

Have you been treated well? Everyone has bad days, but if people at the institution have consistently exhibited bad form during the application and interview process, there is no reason to believe they will treat you better once you are locked into a contract. Past behavior is the best predictor of future behavior.

NEGOTIATING: YES, YOU REALLY HAVE TO DO IT

Leaving graduate school, I was broke. After getting engaged, I had to buy some big-ticket items on credit—in case you haven't heard, diamond rings and honeymoons are expensive. When negotiations with my first employer started, I had little money in the bank and an increasingly bleak credit card balance. Also, I had never talked to another human being about how to negotiate a job offer. Learning to negotiate seemed less important than learning how to teach and do research. Plus, negotiation just felt icky. Naïve, proud, and uncomfortable with the whole process, the only things I negotiated for in my new contract were computers for a lab and moving expenses; this mistake probably cost me tens of thousands of dollars.

Yes, you have to negotiate. The starting offer is just that, a *starting* offer, and it is expected and normal that you make a counteroffer—here, I will cite way more sources than I need to just to hammer home the point (Darley & Zanna, 2004; Horner et al., 2001; Huang-Pollock & Mikami, 2007; Iacono, 1981; Kelsky, 2015; Sternberg, 2004; Vick et al., 2016; Wells et al., 2013). Your initial salary represents a starting point that stays with you throughout your career; even if you get a raise later, it is still based on that initial number. Plus, it may be years before you are in the position to negotiate higher pay.

The importance of negotiation is easier to understand using actual numbers. If you lose out on $4,000 by not negotiating initial salary, then adjusting for a 3% raise each year, that adds up to a loss of $31,300 in the 7 years until tenure (Huang-Pollock & Mikami, 2007). So, you can avoid the hassle of negotiating, or you can buy a new Volkswagen Golf. I know which I would choose.

How to Negotiate

If there is just one thing to remember about negotiating, it is this: You do not have the job yet. Bad form during negotiations can lead to the reconsideration of a candidate's fit for a position (Kelsky, 2015; Vick et al., 2016). Put simply, the offer can be pulled. Anecdotes suggest that rescinded offers are often about candidates trying to negotiate as if they are at a doctoral university when that is not the culture they are entering. If you have just spent months talking about your undying love of teaching to faculty and administrators at a teaching-focused college, does it make sense to start demanding release-time from teaching and thousands of dollars in research start-up costs? Making demands that do not fit the college can lead administrators to withdraw offers due to newfound perceptions of a poor fit. Other behaviors that can sour an offer include lying, being unprofessional, and dragging out the process to wait for a better offer. As in all professional situations, be collegial because you are going to be working with these people for a long time.

Another reason for keeping in mind that you do not have the job yet is that nothing is final until you have it in writing. Do not start contacting other colleges to let them know you are off the market until you have signed a contract, because only then are you truly off the market. Also, it is nice to hear verbal assurances that you will teach two courses a semester, that travel funds are always plentiful, or that your laboratory will have new computers, but you need such assurances to be contractual. No, I do not think that it is typical for administrators to try and take advantage of new faculty, but budgets get cut, administrators change, and people forget things; the only way to ensure that you get what you are promised is to stipulate it in a contract.

Negotiating Salary

Negotiating salary is a game. The object of the game is to guess how much money the college is willing to invest in you as new faculty member. There are some tools to help job candidates make rough guesses about what constitutes a fair offer. *The Chronicle of Higher Education*, the American Association of University Professors Faculty Compensation Survey, and the American Psychological Association's (APA's) Center for Workforce studies all publish information about average salaries by rank at specific universities. For state universities, every employee's salary is public information; this leads to the comical but infuriating factoid that athletic coaches are the highest paid public employees in 39 states (Gaines, 2016). When considering salary data, remember that averages are affected by many factors besides what new psychology professors make, so interpret with caution.

No matter what the initial offer is, ask for more. That is the cardinal rule of the negotiation game. Asking for an increase of 5% to 15% is standard (Kelsky, 2015). However, asking does not always mean getting. Administrators must deal with salaries that are already established and salary compression (Kelsky, 2015; Wells et al., 2013). That is, even if you are worth the money, they are loath to pay a starting assistant professor more than an associate professor who has been there for years. Also, some standardized contracts and union rules stipulate unvarying salary regimens. Community colleges frequently have strict salary guidelines; in general, the negotiation game is played less frequently at community colleges and will only include salary when it does occur (Jenkins, 2013; Twombly, 2004). For part-time positions, pay will be course-based and ineligible for negotiation. Finally, at some institutions, you are not being gamed; they simply do not have the money to pay as well as faculty would like and cannot afford to be generous with salaries.

Negotiating Start-Up Costs

Some would argue that at research-focused institutions start-up cost, not salary, is the most important point of negotiation. After all, graduate assistants, lab space, and equipment are major factors in determining whether you can succeed in a position, and salary does not matter if you do not get tenure. Depending on the institution, requests for start-up costs may be completely unheard of or highly formalized. At community colleges and baccalaureate colleges with modest scholarship requirements, there may be no money set aside for faculty start-up costs. In contrast, at doctoral universities, negotiation will start with the submission of an itemized budget (Huang-Pollock & Mikami, 2007; Sternberg, 2017; Vick et al., 2016). Mentors in your research area will have suggestions for what to request and how much it will cost.

Research conducted by APA illustrates what faculty typically request when entering new positions in psychology departments with graduate programs (Hart, Finno, Kohout, & Wicherski, 2009). Starting with the amount requested, the value of start-up packages for new hires ranged $1,500 to $1,000,000, with a median of $63,715. Before writing up a budget for a cool million, keep in mind that these were all faculty starting new positions, not necessarily new assistant professors. Established faculty can negotiate better deals. What items did faculty request? The most common items were as follows: equipment (52%), travel funds (37%), summer salary (36%), graduate assistant pay (31%), supplies (22%), professional development (17%), and pay for subjects (15%). New faculty also negotiated for their research space, and the average lab was 392 square feet. To make sure that your needs are met, consult with research mentors in writing up a budget for your start-up costs.

Other Negotiable Items

New faculty can benefit from negotiating more than salary and start-up costs. Start dates can be negotiable. No one is going to let you start in the middle of a semester, but starting earlier or later may be an option. Although not as sexy as a big pay increase, negotiating better benefits is tantamount to an increase in pay because it is money that eventually ends up back in your hands. Negotiating a reduced teaching load can be useful in freeing up time to focus on starting a research program. Professional fees are quite expensive, and you can ask for money to cover them. Similarly, if you are in a field where licensure is expected, consider negotiating release time and funding to help with this ongoing professional responsibility (Matthews, 2000). Moving expenses can be useful when starting out, but remember that moving expenses are a one-time payout and getting a $1,000 salary bump will ultimately be much more valuable than many thousands in moving expenses. One final negotiation issue is the hiring of a partner (i.e., spousal hire). Experts agree that negotiations are the best chance you have to get an institution to hire your partner, but these types of deals are mostly limited to large, elite institutions (Huang-Pollock & Mikami, 2007; Sternberg, 2017; Wells et al., 2013).

DEALING WITH DECLINED OFFERS AND REJECTIONS

After months of hard work, you have done your negotiations and signed your contract. What is your reward? You get to tell other search committees that you are off the market. Let the search chair at places you interviewed in person know that you have accepted an offer so that they can factor it into their own deliberations and negotiations (Vick et al., 2016). Professional courtesy dictates that you do this as soon as possible; this is especially true if they are waiting to hear back about an offer they made to you because any delay reduces their chances of making a hire.

Alternatively, after months of hard work, you have gotten no offers good enough to accept or no offers at all. What do you do now? Rejection letters are not a rejection of you or of your worth as a psychologist; the only thing they mean is that the fit was not as good with you as it was with someone else (Darley & Zanna, 2004). All you can do in response is find a better fit or make yourself a better fit.

Becoming a better fit requires time and work. If funding is available, you can stay in graduate school another year. Your luck may change with the next round of open positions. However, aimless lingering in grad school does not guarantee employment; be intentional about pushing projects toward publication, obtaining teaching experience, gathering new skills, and contributing meaningful service. Graduate school can work as an investment in future potential on the job market, but the relative return on that investment diminishes the longer it takes to graduate. In other words, graduate after, at most, 7 years whether or not you have landed your dream job.

Another option for becoming a better fit is to obtain a postdoctoral position. Postdocs lead to additional research skills and publications, and these are the qualities that separate hires from nonhires at many institutions. However, postdocs without a teaching emphasis do not increase fit for positions at most community colleges or baccalaureate colleges; in fact, spending a year or two doing nothing but research makes candidates seem like a poorer fit.

The final option for strengthening yourself as a candidate, assuming that you were going for full-time, tenure-track positions, is to obtain work as a visiting professor, instructor, or adjunct. Such positions tend to focus narrowly on instruction. If teaching experience is what you need to bolster your CV, then these positions can be useful, but they are more likely to hurt than help your chances of getting research done. As such, the experience you get in non–tenure-track jobs is unlikely to increase fit for positions at doctoral universities.

It is midterm, and I just had to have "the talk" with students in one of my more challenging classes, several of whom are failing. I said to them,

> Most of the points are still available in this class, so there is a lot of room to move your grade around. If you have been successful, then keep doing what you are doing. If you are not happy with your grade, then something has to change in the second half of the semester. It's not going to be me. It's not going to be the quizzes or papers. Your behavior has to change.

This same talk applies to becoming and being a psychology professor. If you have been successful so far—tons of pubs, great teaching evals, prestigious service—keep up the good work as you are launching your faculty career. If your efforts have not garnered interviews and offers, something has to change. One way performance on the job market is different from performance in a class, however, is that you can change your goals. Faculty life can be rewarding in all types of positions at all types of colleges and universities—are you aiming for the right ones? I have even heard that careers exist outside of academia, but I cannot personally confirm or deny that fact. After all, I am a psychology professor, and my goal is for you to be one too.

Epilogue

"OK, this is not working. If you all can't come up with a research project, I'll just have to come up with an alternative assignment. Class is over." That is what I was about to say. A career first, I was about to walk out in the middle of class.

The students, working in small groups, had been sharing their ideas for naturalistic studies for the last 30 minutes of research methods. Now the groups were sharing their best ideas with the whole class so that we could pick one to conduct as large group. It was an opportunity for the students to do real research with the world as their laboratory, and the only limitation was their creativity in operationalizing psychological concepts using observable phenomena. What did they come up with?

"We're going to count how many people pay for their lunches with cash or credit cards."

"Our plan is to see if people look up from their phones when walking across campus."

"We're going to time how long it takes people to get food and then see if they eat it at the café or to-go. Plus see if there is a sex difference."

To understate things, I found their ideas to be lacking. No one ever accused me of having a good poker face, and sensing my verdict on their ideas, the students completely shut down. No more discussion. No more brainstorming. No more thinking at all. To make up for their disengagement, I tossed out idea after idea, my voice getting higher and higher, louder and louder, silences getting longer and longer.

http://dx.doi.org/10.1037/0000152-010
Becoming a Psychology Professor: Your Guide to Landing the Right Academic Job,
by G. A. Boysen

"OK, this is not working. . . . Class is over." I almost said it. Instead, what came out was, "Go back to your small groups for a few more minutes and try to build on these ideas." And then I walked out.

I came back after taking a moment to recuperate, and the class did eventually produce a workable idea for a study. Nonetheless, I failed as a teacher that day. Believe it or not, I share this story not as some cautionary tale but to illustrate some final positive messages about being professor.

IT'S ALL ABOUT FIT

If you learn just one thing from this book, it should be that becoming a successful professor of psychology is all about fit. Being a professor must fit your temperament, interests, and talents. Like any other job, some people are cut out for it and some people are not.

Going back to my classroom failure, you might reasonably wonder if I am cut out to be a professor. However, I see that class period, frustrating as it was, as a perfect illustration of the control I have over my work: I set the class goals, selected the teaching methods, evaluated the success of the lesson, and decided how I would teach it the next time around. That is the essence of academic freedom—self-direction of teaching, research, and service—and there is no other characteristic of being a professor that is a better match for me. For you, perhaps it is the prestige, flexibility, intellectual rigor, collegiate environment, or some other factor that is a good match, but career satisfaction will be elusive without that all-important fit.

The idea of fit with "being a professor" is somewhat of a misnomer because the job varies so dramatically from position to position, and this means that fit with your specific job is also essential. Like a car stereo with "bass," "treble," and "mid" knobs for adjusting music to your taste, different positions allow you to adjust your levels of teaching, research, and service. My wife turns the bass down, and I turn it up; for this reason, and a host of other preferences for which there is no right answer, we drive separate cars. Likewise, most grad students want to be professors, but some want to crank up the research, others want to crank up the teaching, and some want balance—they end up in different positions at different colleges.

The fact that there were only 12 students enrolled in that research methods class made it harder, not easier, to give up that day. Because of that small number, I knew the group dynamics of each discussion team, I knew who probably had great ideas but was too shy to share them, I knew who had no idea what we were talking about, and I knew a host of other stuff about the students—some of it academic, some it not. A small class size also meant that I could have students do real research and write it up as an empirical report. Students could learn by doing psychology rather than listening to me talk about it in a lecture hall. Moreover, how I interacted with those 12 students, and the students in my other courses, was the main determinant of whether I would be promoted and tenured. All of this is exactly how I wanted it to be because I was in a tenure-track position at a college that fit my professional priorities. If you do not want to be tempted to give up when work gets tough, then make sure that you are in a position that matches your priorities too.

START EARLY

You may know that being a professor is a good fit for you and you may have the perfect college picked out, but you still have to beat out other aspiring professors for that dream job. The people who get a chance to interview for your dream job will be those who have accumulated the most impressive and consistent professional records. Creating such a record takes years and years. So, another lesson you should take away from this book is that it pays to start early on the path toward being a professor.

Although walking out of class to recuperate from my poorly executed lesson was not my finest hour, I was still teaching the class I wanted at the college I wanted. How did that happen? My second summer in graduate school, the director of undergraduate education called and asked if I wanted to take over a learning and memory course the next month—not my specialty area, never taught a full course, no time to prepare. I leapt at the chance. Grad students were not supposed to teach that early in the program, but I did, and it led me to teach Intro to Psych the next summer, Abnormal the next year, and Research Methods after that. By the time I was sending out applications, that early start had allowed me to teach as many courses as some assistant professors, and I was ready to compete for jobs.

Another reason to start early is that it takes a long time to get good at being a professor. Teaching is hard. Research is hard. Honest and non-delusional psychologists will admit that they still have a lot to learn about teaching and research no matter how far along they are in their careers. Now imagine how much room there is for improvement at the start of a career. If you care about being a good psychology professor—and how else would you have gotten this far in the book?—then start mastering your craft as early as possible.

One of the reasons I was so frustrated by the Research Methods students' inability to come up with a decent research idea was because it was so easy for me to do so. I cannot interact with another human being without thinking, "Hey, that's an idea for a study!" Why was it easy for me and hard for them? It was because I had been coming up with study ideas since my first semester of graduate school. From a teaching standpoint, why persist with the class even though I was frustrated with the students' inability to meet my expectations for thinking like good little psychologists? The reason is that I had experiences going all the way back to that very first learning and memory course, illustrating that no matter how obvious something seems to me as a teacher, it is always much, much harder for the students. Being a competent teacher and researcher only comes with time and repetition— practice starts now.

THE BEST JOB IN THE WORLD

The final point is that, for me, being a psychology professor is the best job in the world. Psychology is endlessly fascinating and productive. What could be more enjoyable or rewarding than professing it to others through teaching and research?

Ultimately, I kept at it with those students because I cared. The concepts I was trying to teach were important, interesting, and useful, and I wanted to give the students a chance to benefit from understanding them. This motivation extends beyond one class, however. Be it through teaching, research, or service, I care about expanding people's knowledge and use of psychology. If you agree, then being a psychology professor may be the best job in the world for you as well.

Appendix

JOB SEARCH TIMELINE

ONE YEAR BEFORE APPLYING

☐ Construct a CV.

☐ Make plans to gather additional teaching, scholarship, or service experiences to round out your CV.

☐ Attend job talks and other interview events in your department.

☐ Network with mentors working in the type of position you plan to seek.

☐ Begin discussions of your career goals with potential letter of recommendation writers.

☐ Invite potential letter writers to review your research, and/or your teaching.

☐ Attempt to arrange a schedule for the upcoming year that will allow you the flexibility to work extensively on application materials and go on interviews.

SIX MONTHS BEFORE APPLYING

☐ Conduct an honest self-evaluation of your CV and decide (a) if you have the qualifications to go on the market, (b) what positions you are most qualified for, and (c) if there are any holes in your CV that can be filled in the next 6 months.

☐ Meet with mentors, inform them of your intention to apply for jobs the next school year, and solicit advice.

☐ Ensure that your dissertation can be finished in advance of starting a position in approximately 15 months.

☐ Make a final decision to go on the market.

THREE MONTHS BEFORE APPLYING

☐ Write and edit multiple drafts of your application materials.

☐ Update any professional webpages and social media webpages to reflect your recent accomplishments and central messages of your application materials.

☐ Officially ask letter of reference writers if they know your work well enough to provide you with a strong recommendation letter.

☐ Start planning a research presentation, and/or teaching demonstration.

☐ Create accounts and automatic alerts on job websites.

☐ Start to monitor advertisements and identify matching positions.

TWO MONTHS BEFORE APPLYING

☐ Create an organizational/filing system to keep track of job advertisements, applications, institutional information, and communications about the jobs.

☐ Start researching positions as they are announced, saving the notes for later reference when preparing for interviews.

☐ Have multiple peers and mentors review and provide feedback on your application materials.

☐ Meet with letter writers to (a) go over the types of institutions you will be applying to, (b) ask their preferences for receiving requests for letters to be sent, and (c) provide them with (semi-)final versions of your application materials.

ONE MONTH BEFORE APPLYING

☐ Make the final selection of positions.

☐ Provide mentors with a spreadsheet containing position information, institution information, deadlines, and addresses for submission.

☐ Request transcripts as required for applications.

☐ Obtain letterhead for cover letters.

☐ Write final drafts of cover letters for each position that contain accurate, personalized information about the institution and position requirements.

☐ Make edits, as needed, to other application materials to better fit positions.

☐ Continue to monitor job advertisements for newly announced positions.

☐ Start to craft answers to typical interview questions.

☐ Buy professional but comfortable clothes for video and in-person interviews.

☐ Conduct mock interviews and practice answers to standard interview questions.

BEFORE THE DEADLINE

☐ Submit the exact materials required for each position.

AFTER SUBMISSION OF MATERIALS

☐ Continue to monitor job advertisements for newly announced positions.

☐ Monitor for communications from search committees and reply promptly to requests for information or interviews.

AFTER INTERVIEW INVITATIONS

☐ Conduct detailed research on institutions and people before the interview.

☐ Prepare answers to interview questions that are specific to each institution.

☐ Conduct initial screening interviews via phone and/or video.

☐ Conduct on-campus interviews.

AFTER INTERVIEWS ARE COMPLETE

☐ If you found a job: Negotiate your contract and begin planning for the transition.

☐ If you did not find a job: Continue to monitor for late-emerging positions if you have no offers from the first round of applications, and evaluate whether the remaining open positions are acceptable or if you will restart the application process next year.

References

Adams, K. A. (2002). *What colleges and universities want in new faculty*. Washington, DC: Association of American Colleges & Universities. Retrieved from http://files.eric.ed.gov/fulltext/ED472499.pdf

American Association of Community Colleges. (2016). *2016 fact sheet*. Retrieved from https://www.napicaacc.com/docs/AACC_Fact_Sheet_2016.pdf

American Association of University Professors. (n.d.). *Shared governance*. Retrieved from https://www.aaup.org/our-programs/shared-governance

American Association of University Professors. (2014). *Contingent appointments and the academic profession*. Retrieved from https://www.aaup.org/report/contingent-appointments-and-academic-profession

American Association of University Professors. (2017). *Trends in the academic labor force, 1975–2015*. Retrieved from https://www.aaup.org/sites/default/files/Academic%20Labor%20Force%20Trends%201975-2015.pdf

American Psychological Association. (n.d.-a). *Community college fact sheet*. Retrieved from https://www.apa.org/ed/precollege/undergrad/ptacc/fact-sheet.pdf

American Psychological Association. (n.d.-b). *Valuing diversity in faculty: A guide*. Retrieved from http://www.apa.org/pi/oema/resources/brochures/valuing-diversity.aspx

American Psychological Association. (2009). *Graduate faculty in psychology interested in lesbian, gay, bisexual, and transgender issues 2009 survey*. Retrieved from http://www.apa.org/pi/lgbt/resources/survey/index.aspx

American Psychological Association. (2010). *APAGS resource guide for ethnic minority graduate students*. Retrieved from https://www.apa.org/apags/resources/ethnic-minority-guide.pdf

Anziano, M. C., & Burke, B. L. (2014). Landing your first job: Finding your ideal fit. In J. N. Busler, B. C. Beins, & W. Buskist (Eds.), *Preparing the new psychology professoriate: Helping graduate students become competent teachers* (2nd ed., pp. 191–197). Washington, DC: Society for the Teaching of Psychology. Retrieved from http://teachpsych.org/Resources/Documents/ebooks/pnpp2014.pdf

Ault, R. L. (2014). Four desirable qualities for teaching at a small liberal arts college. In J. N. Busler, B. C. Beins, & W. Buskist (Eds.), *Preparing the new psychology professoriate: Helping graduate students become competent teachers* (2nd ed., pp. 167–169). Washington, DC: Society for the Teaching of Psychology. Retrieved from http://teachpsych.org/Resources/Documents/ebooks/pnpp2014.pdf

Bartlett, T. (2017, March 17). Spoiled science. *The Chronicle of Higher Education*. Retrieved from https://www.chronicle.com/article/Spoiled-Science/239529

Beers, M. J., Hill, J. C., & Thompson, C. A. (2012). *The STP guide to graduate training programs in the teaching of psychology* (2nd ed.). Washington, DC: Society for the Teaching of Psychology. Retrieved from http://teachpsych.org/ebooks/gst2012/index.php

Benson, T. A., & Buskist, W. (2005). Understanding "excellence in teaching" as assessed by psychology faculty search committees. *Teaching of Psychology, 32,* 47–49.

Boyd, B., Caraway, S. J., & Flores Niemann, Y. (2017). *Surviving and thriving in academia: A guide for members of marginalized groups.* Washington, DC: American Psychological Association. Retrieved from http://www.apa.org/pi/oema/resources/brochures/surviving.pdf

Boysen, G. A. (2011). The prevalence and predictors of teaching courses in doctoral psychology programs. *Teaching of Psychology, 38,* 49–52. http://dx.doi.org/10.1177/0098628310390850

Boysen, G. A. (2016). Using student evaluations to improve teaching: Evidence-based recommendations. *Scholarship of Teaching and Learning in Psychology, 2,* 273–284. http://dx.doi.org/10.1037/stl0000069

Boysen, G. A., Jones, C., Kaltwasser, R., & Thompson, E. (2018). Keys to a successful job talk: Perceptions of psychology faculty. *Teaching of Psychology, 45,* 270–277. http://dx.doi.org/10.1177/0098628318779277

Boysen, G. A., Morton, J., & Nieves, T. (in press). Kisses of death in the hiring of psychology faculty. *Teaching of Psychology.*

Brakke, K. (2014). New faculty as colleagues and change agents. In J. N. Busler, B. C. Beins, & W. Buskist (Eds.), *Preparing the new psychology professoriate: Helping graduate students become competent teachers* (2nd ed., pp. 139–143). Washington, DC: Society for the Teaching of Psychology. Retrieved from http://teachpsych.org/Resources/Documents/ebooks/pnpp2014.pdf

Braxton, J. M., & Lyken-Segosebe, D. (2015). Community college faculty engagement in Boyer's domains of scholarship. *New Directions for Community Colleges, 2015*(171), 7–14. http://dx.doi.org/10.1002/cc.20150

Brems, C., Lampman, C., & Johnson, M. E. (1995). Preparation of applications for academic positions in psychology. *American Psychologist, 50,* 533–537. http://dx.doi.org/10.1037/0003-066X.50.7.533

Buddie, A. M. (2014). The successful job applicant at Kennesaw State University. In J. N. Busler, B. C. Beins, & W. Buskist (Eds.), *Preparing the new psychology professoriate: Helping graduate students become competent teachers* (2nd ed., pp. 162–166). Washington, DC: Society for the Teaching of Psychology. Retrieved from http://teachpsych.org/Resources/Documents/ebooks/pnpp2014.pdf

Bureau of Labor Statistics. (2015). *Postsecondary teachers.* Retrieved from https://www.bls.gov/ooh/education-training-and-library/postsecondary-teachers.htm

Buskist, W., Tears, R. S., Davis, S. F., & Rodrigue, K. M. (2002). The teaching of psychology course: Prevalence and content. *Teaching of Psychology, 29,* 140–142.

Byrnes, J. P. (2007). Publishing trends of psychology faculty during their pretenure years. *Psychological Science, 18,* 283–286. http://dx.doi.org/10.1111/j.1467-9280.2007.01889.x

Carnegie Classification of Institutions of Higher Education. (2016). *2015 update: Facts & figures.* Retrieved from http://carnegieclassifications.iu.edu/downloads/CCIHE2015-FactsFigures.pdf

Center for Community College Student Engagement. (2016). *Community college faculty survey of student engagement.* Retrieved from http://www.ccsse.org/survey/CCFSSE/CCFSSE2016_cohort_freqs_faconly.pdf

The Chronicle of Higher Education. (2017, August 13). The Almanac of Higher Education: 2017–18. Retrieved from https://www.chronicle.com/specialreport/The-Almanac-of-Higher/132

Clark, R. A., Harden, S. L., & Johnson, W. B. (2000). Mentor relationships in clinical psychology doctoral training: Results of a national survey. *Teaching of Psychology, 27,* 262–268. http://dx.doi.org/10.1207/S15328023TOP2704_04

Clifton, J., & Buskist, W. (2005). Preparing graduate students for academic positions in psychology: Suggestions from job advertisements. *Teaching of Psychology, 32,* 265–267.

Cone, J. D., & Foster, S. L. (2006). *Dissertations and theses from start to finish: Psychology and related fields* (2nd ed.). Washington, DC: American Psychological Association.

Cope, C., Michalski, D. S., & Fowler, G. A. (2016). *Summary report: Tuition and financial aid.* Washington, DC: American Psychological Association. Retrieved from www.apa.org/ed/graduate

Critchfield, T. S., & Jordan, J. S. (2014). Finding faculty who fit at a large mid-level public university: General and institution-specific considerations. In J. N. Busler, B. C. Beins, & W. Buskist (Eds.), *Preparing the new psychology professoriate: Helping graduate students become competent teachers* (2nd ed., pp. 170–176). Washington, DC: Society for the Teaching of Psychology. Retrieved from http://teachpsych.org/Resources/Documents/ebooks/pnpp2014.pdf

Darley, J. M., & Zanna, M. P. (2004). The hiring process in academia. In J. M. Darley, M. P. Zanna, & H. L. Roediger (Eds.), *The compleat academic:*

A career guide (2nd ed., pp. 31–56). Washington, DC: American Psychological Association.

Demaray, M. K., Carlson, J. S., & Hodgson, K. K. (2003). Assistant professors of school psychology: A national survey of program directors and job applicants. *Psychology in the Schools, 40,* 691–698. http://dx.doi.org/10.1002/pits.10130

Desrochers, D. M., & Kirshstein, R. (2014). *Labor intensive or labor expensive? Changing staffing and compensation patterns in higher education.* Washington, DC: American Institutes for Research. Retrieved from http://www.air.org/sites/default/files/downloads/report/DeltaCostAIR-Labor-Expensive-Higher-Education-Staffing-Brief-Feb2014.pdf

Dickinson, S. C., & Johnson, W. B. (2000). Mentoring in clinical psychology doctoral programs: A national survey of directors of training. *The Clinical Supervisor, 19,* 137–152. http://dx.doi.org/10.1300/J001v19n01_08

Dunn, D. S., & Zaremba, S. B. (1997). Thriving at liberal arts colleges: The more compleat academic. *Teaching of Psychology, 24,* 8–14. http://dx.doi.org/10.1177/009862839702400104

Eby, L. T., Allen, T. D., Evans, S. C., Ng, T., & DuBois, D. (2008). Does mentoring matter? A multidisciplinary meta-analysis comparing mentored and non-mentored individuals. *Journal of Vocational Behavior, 72,* 254–267. http://dx.doi.org/10.1016/j.jvb.2007.04.005

Ewing, A. T. (2014). Characteristics of successful community college academicians. In J. N. Busler, B. C. Beins, & W. Buskist (Eds.), *Preparing the new psychology professoriate: Helping graduate students become competent teachers* (2nd ed., pp. 121–126). Washington, DC: Society for the Teaching of Psychology. Retrieved from http://teachpsych.org/Resources/Documents/ebooks/pnpp2014.pdf

Fals-Stewart, W. (1996). Applications for academic positions in psychology: Recommendations for search committees. *American Psychologist, 51,* 737–738. http://dx.doi.org/10.1037/0003-066X.51.7.737

Follette, V., & Klesges, R. C. (1988). Academic employment: A longitudinal study of the recruiting process and hired applicants. *Professional Psychology: Research and Practice, 19,* 345–348. http://dx.doi.org/10.1037/0735-7028.19.3.345

Franklin, J. (2001). Interpreting the numbers: Using a narrative to help others read student evaluations of your teaching accurately. *New Directions for Teaching and Learning, 2001,* 85–100. http://dx.doi.org/10.1002/tl.10001

Franz, S., Manbur, M., & Neufeld, G. (2014). Highline College: A diverse community college. In J. N. Busler, B. C. Beins, & W. Buskist (Eds.), *Preparing the new psychology professoriate: Helping graduate students become competent teachers* (2nd ed., pp. 132–143). Washington, DC: Society for the Teaching of Psychology. Retrieved from http://teachpsych.org/Resources/Documents/ebooks/pnpp2014.pdf

Fugate, A. L., & Amey, M. J. (2000). Career stages of community college faculty: Qualitative analysis of their career paths, roles, and development. *Community College Review, 28*, 1–22. http://dx.doi.org/10.1177/009155210002800101

Gaines, C. (2016, September 22). 39 US states where the highest-paid public employee is a college coach. *Business Insider*. Retrieved from http://www.businessinsider.com/us-states-highest-paid-public-employee-college-coach-2016-9

Gore, P. A., Jr., Murdock, N. L., & Haley, S. J. (1998). Entering the ivory tower: Characteristics of successful counseling psychology faculty applicants. *The Counseling Psychologist, 26*, 640–657. http://dx.doi.org/10.1177/0011000098264007

Hart, B., Finno, A., Kohout, J., & Wicherski, M. (2009). *2008–09: APA survey of graduate departments of psychology*. Washington, DC: American Psychological Association. Retrieved from http://www.apa.org/workforce/publications/grad-09/index.aspx

Henderson, B. B. (2011). Publishing patterns at state comprehensive universities: The changing nature of faculty work and the quest for status. *Journal of the Professoriate, 5*, 35–66.

Henderson, B. B., & Buchanan, H. E. (2007). The scholarship of teaching and learning: A special niche for faculty at comprehensive universities? *Research in Higher Education, 48*, 523–543. http://dx.doi.org/10.1007/s11162-006-9035-2

Horner, S. L., Pape, S. J., & O'Connor, E. A. (2001). Drs. Strangelove or: How we learned to stop worrying and love the job search process. *Educational Psychology Review, 13*, 53–69. http://dx.doi.org/10.1023/A:1009056918293

Huang-Pollock, C. L., & Mikami, A. Y. (2007). The academic job search: Time line, tips, and tactics. *The Behavior Therapist, 30*, 104–108.

Hurlburt, S., & McGarrah, M. (2017). *The shifting academic workforce: Where are the contingent faculty?* Washington, DC: American Institutes for Research. Retrieved from http://www.air.org/sites/default/files/downloads/report/Shifting-Academic-Workforce-November-2016.pdf

Hurtado, S., Eagan, K., Pryor, J. H., Whang, H., & Tran, S. (2011). *Undergraduate teaching faculty: The 2010–2011 HERI Faculty Survey*. Los Angeles, CA: Higher Education Research Institute.

Iacono, W. G. (1981). The academic job search: The experiences of a new PhD in the job market. *Canadian Psychology, 22*, 217–227. http://dx.doi.org/10.1037/h0081167

Jenkins, R. (2003, December 12). Applying for jobs at two-year colleges. *The Chronicle of Higher Education*. Retrieved from https://www.chronicle.com/article/Applying-for-Jobs-at-Two-Year/45289

Jenkins, R. (2004a, April 12). A foot in the door at community colleges. *The Chronicle of Higher Education*. Retrieved from https://www.chronicle.com/article/A-Foot-in-the-Door-at/44561

Jenkins, R. (2004b, January 15). Interviewing at a two-year college. *The Chronicle of Higher Education*. Retrieved from https://www.chronicle.com/article/Interviewing-at-a-Two-Year/44744

Jenkins, R. (2013, November 18). How the job search differs at community colleges. *The Chronicle of Higher Education*. Retrieved from https://www.chronicle.com/article/How-the-Job-Search-Differs-at/143089

Jenkins, R. (2014, February 14). Cattle call. *The Chronicle of Higher Education*. Retrieved from https://www.chronicle.com/article/Cattle-Call/45103

Jenkins, R. (2018, March 23). What to expect at a community-college interview. *The Chronicle of Higher Education*. Retrieved from https://www.chronicle.com/article/What-to-Expect-at-a/242578

John, L. K., Loewenstein, G., & Prelec, D. (2012). Measuring the prevalence of questionable research practices with incentives for truth telling. *Psychological Science, 23*, 524–532. http://dx.doi.org/10.1177/0956797611430953

Johnson, W. B. (2002). The intentional mentor: Strategies and guidelines for the practice of mentoring. *Professional Psychology: Research and Practice, 33*, 88–96. http://dx.doi.org/10.1037/0735-7028.33.1.88

Johnson, W. B., & Huwe, J. M. (2003). *Getting mentored in graduate school*. Washington, DC: American Psychological Association.

Joy, S. (2006). What should I be doing, and where are they doing it? Scholarly productivity of academic psychologists. *Perspectives on Psychological Science, 1*, 346–364. http://dx.doi.org/10.1111/j.1745-6916.2006.00020.x

Juszkiewicz, J. (2016). *Trends in community college enrollment and completion data 2016*. Washington, DC: American Association of Community Colleges. Retrieved from https://www.aacc.nche.edu/wp-content/uploads/2017/11/TrendsCCEnrollment_Final2016.pdf

Keith, K. D., & Zwokinski, J. (2014). Won't you be my neighbor? Making yourself an excellent faculty candidate. In J. N. Busler, B. C. Beins, & W. Buskist (Eds.), *Preparing the new psychology professoriate: Helping graduate students become competent teachers* (2nd ed., pp. 198–204). Washington, DC: Society for the Teaching of Psychology. Retrieved from http://teachpsych.org/Resources/Documents/ebooks/pnpp2014.pdf

Kelsky, K. (2015). *The professor is in: The essential guide to turning your Ph.D. into a job*. New York, NY: Three Rivers.

Kuther, T. L. (2008). *Surviving graduate school in psychology: A pocket mentor*. Washington, DC: American Psychological Association.

Landrum, R. E., & Clump, M. A. (2004). Departmental search committees and the evaluation of faculty applicants. *Teaching of Psychology, 31*, 12–17. http://dx.doi.org/10.1207/s15328023top3101_4

Lewis, K. G. (2001). Making sense of student written comments. *New Directions for Teaching and Learning, 2001*(87), 25–32. http://dx.doi.org/10.1002/tl.25

Lord, C. G. (2004). A guide to PhD graduate school: How they keep score in the big leagues. In J. M. Darley, M. P. Zanna, & H. L. Roediger (Eds.), *The compleat academic: A career guide* (2nd ed., pp. 3–15). Washington, DC: American Psychological Association.

Marston, S. H., & Brunetti, G. J. (2009). Job satisfaction of experienced professors at a liberal arts college. *Education, 130*, 323–347.

Matthews, J. R. (2000). Special issues facing new faculty with doctorates in applied subfields. *Teaching of Psychology, 27*, 216–217.

McDermott, K. B., & Braver, T. S. (2004). After graduate school: A faculty position or a postdoctoral fellowship? In J. M. Darley, M. P. Zanna, & H. L. Roediger (Eds.), *The compleat academic: A career guide* (2nd ed., pp. 17–30). Washington, DC: American Psychological Association.

McElroy, H. K., & Prentice-Dunn, S. (2005). Graduate students' perceptions of a teaching of psychology course. *Teaching of Psychology, 32*, 123–125.

Meizlish, D., & Kaplan, M. (2008). Valuing and evaluating teaching in academic hiring: A multidisciplinary, cross-institutional study. *The Journal of Higher Education, 79*, 489–512. http://dx.doi.org/10.1080/00221546.2008.11772114

Meyers, S. A., & Prieto, L. R. (2000). Training in the teaching of psychology: What is done and examining the differences. *Teaching of Psychology, 27*, 258–261. http://dx.doi.org/10.1207/S15328023TOP2704_03

Michalski, D., Kohout, J., Wicherski, M., & Hart, B. (2011). *2009 doctorate employment survey*. Washington, DC: American Psychological Association. Retrieved from http://www.apa.org/workforce/publications/09-doc-empl/report.pdf

Milem, J. F., Berger, J. B., & Dey, E. L. (2000). Faculty time allocation: A study of change over twenty years. *The Journal of Higher Education, 71*, 454–475. http://dx.doi.org/10.1080/00221546.2000.11778845

Miller, H. L., Flores, D., & Tait, V. (2014). Prospects for the new professoriate at Brigham Young University. In J. N. Busler, B. C. Beins, & W. Buskist (Eds.), *Preparing the new psychology professoriate: Helping graduate students become competent teachers* (2nd ed., pp. 158–161). Washington, DC: Society for the Teaching of Psychology. Retrieved from http://teachpsych.org/Resources/Documents/ebooks/pnpp2014.pdf

Miller, R. L. (2014). What comprehensive primarily undergraduate institutions look for when hiring new faculty. In J. N. Busler, B. C. Beins, & W. Buskist (Eds.), *Preparing the new psychology professoriate: Helping graduate students become competent teachers* (2nd ed., pp. 205–208). Washington, DC: Society for the Teaching of Psychology. Retrieved from http://teachpsych.org/Resources/Documents/ebooks/pnpp2014.pdf

Morgan, E. M., & Landrum, R. E. (2012). *You've earned your doctorate in psychology . . . now what? Securing a job as an academic or professional psychologist*. Washington, DC: American Psychological Association.

Morphew, C., Ward, K., & Wolf-Wendel, L. (2016). *Changes in faculty composition at independent colleges*. The Counsel on Independent Colleges. Retrieved from https://www.cic.edu/r/r/Documents/CIC-Ward-report.pdf

Murray, J. P. (2013). The lack of intentionality in recruiting and hiring of new community college faculty. *Journal of Modern Education Review, 3*, 108–119.

Myers, D. G. (1999). Close relationships and quality of life. In D. Kahneman, E. Diener, & N. Schwarz (Eds.), *Well-being: The foundations of hedonic psychology* (pp. 374–391). New York, NY: Russell Sage Foundation. Retrieved from http://psy2.ucsd.edu/~nchristenfeld/Happiness_Readings_files/Class 8 - Myers 1999.pdf

NACADA: The Global Community for Academic Advising. (n.d.). *2011 National Survey of Academic Advising.* Retrieved from http://www.nacada.ksu.edu/ Resources/Clearinghouse/View-Articles/2011-NACADA-National-Survey.aspx

National Center for Educational Statistics. (1997). *Teaching workload of full-time postsecondary faculty.* Retrieved from https://nces.ed.gov/pubsearch/ pubsinfo.asp?pubid=98002

National Center for Educational Statistics. (2003). *Percentage distribution of full-time faculty and instructional staff in degree-granting postsecondary institutions, by level and control of institution, selected instruction activities, and number of classes taught for credit: Fall 2003.* Retrieved from https://nces.ed.gov/ programs/digest/d15/tables/dt15_315.30.asp

National Center for Educational Statistics. (2017). *Most popular majors.* Retrieved from https://nces.ed.gov/fastfacts/display.asp?id=37

Ng, C. F. (1997). Recruitment practices and job search for academic positions in psychology. *Canadian Psychology, 38,* 25–42. http://dx.doi.org/10.1037/ 0708-5591.38.1.25

O'Meara, K. A. (2007). Striving for what? Exploring the pursuit of prestige. In J. C. Smart (Ed.), *Higher education: Handbook of theory and research* (Vol. 22, pp. 121–179). Dordrecht, The Netherlands: Springer. http:// dx.doi.org/10.1007/978-1-4020-5666-6_3

Orwell, G. (1954). *A collection of essays.* Garden City, NY: Doubleday Anchor.

Pelham, B. (n.d.). *Doing postdoctoral work—Should I?* Retrieved from http:// www.apa.org/careers/resources/academic/postdoc-work.aspx

Provasnik, S., & Planty, M. (2008). *Community colleges: Special supplement to the 2008 condition of education.* Washington, DC: National Center for Education Statistics. Retrieved from https://nces.ed.gov/pubsearch/pubsinfo. asp?pubid=2008033

Richmond, A. S., Boysen, G. A., & Gurung, R. A. R. (2016). *An evidence-based guide to college and university teaching: Developing the model teacher.* New York, NY: Routledge/Taylor & Francis Group. http://dx.doi.org/10.4324/ 9781315642529

Ronson, J. (2016). *So you've been publicly shamed.* New York, NY: Riverhead Books.

Rudmann, J. (2014). Qualities and abilities our psychology department seeks in outstanding job candidates. In J. N. Busler, B. C. Beins, & W. Buskist (Eds.), *Preparing the new psychology professoriate: Helping graduate students become competent teachers* (2nd ed., pp. 113–126). Washington, DC: Society for the Teaching of Psychology. Retrieved from http://teachpsych.org/Resources/ Documents/ebooks/pnpp2014.pdf

Schmaling, K. B., Trevino, A. Y., Lind, J. R., Blume, A. W., & Baker, D. L. (2015). Diversity statements: How faculty applicants address diversity. *Journal of Diversity in Higher Education, 8,* 213–224. http://dx.doi.org/10.1037/a0038549

Schwebel, D. C., & Karver, M. S. (2004). Recent trends in the research-oriented clinical psychology academic job market. *The Behavior Therapist, 27,* 174–179.

Serow, R. C. (2000). Research and teaching at a research university. *Higher Education, 40,* 449–463. http://dx.doi.org/10.1023/A:1004154512833

Sheehan, E. P., & Haselhorst, H. (1999). A profile of applicants for an academic position in social psychology. *Journal of Social Behavior & Personality, 14,* 23–30.

Sheehan, E. P., McDevitt, T. M., & Ross, H. C. (1998). Looking for a job as a psychology professor? Factors affecting applicant success. *Teaching of Psychology, 25,* 8–11. http://dx.doi.org/10.1207/s15328023top2501_3

Sikorski, J. F., & Bruce, E. K. (2014). Successful job applicants at large state universities. In J. N. Busler, B. C. Beins, & W. Buskist (Eds.), *Preparing the new psychology professoriate: Helping graduate students become competent teachers* (2nd ed., pp. 185–190). Washington, DC: Society for the Teaching of Psychology. Retrieved from http://teachpsych.org/Resources/Documents/ebooks/pnpp2014.pdf

Society for the Teaching of Psychology. (2013). *STP taskforce: Documenting model teaching competencies.* Retrieved from http://teachpsych.org/resources/Documents/publications/2013 Model Teaching Competencies.pdf

Society for the Teaching of Psychology, Graduate Student Teaching Association. (2017). *Society for the Teaching of Psychology Graduate Student Teaching Association (GSTA) policies & procedures.* Retrieved from http://teachpsych.org/Resources/Documents/administrative/GSTABylawsOct2017.pdf

Sternberg, R. J. (2004). Obtaining a research grant: The applicant's view. In J. M. Darley, M. P. Zanna, & H. L. Roediger (Eds.), *The compleat academic: A career guide* (2nd ed., pp. 169–184). Washington, DC: American Psychological Association.

Sternberg, R. J. (2017). *Starting your academic career in psychology.* Washington, DC: American Psychological Association. http://dx.doi.org/10.1037/0000013-000

Troisi, J. D., Christopher, A. N., & Batsell, W. R. J. (2014). Ten suggestions for securing a faculty position at a selective liberal arts school. In J. N. Busler, B. C. Beins, & W. Buskist (Eds.), *Preparing the new psychology professoriate: Helping graduate students become competent teachers* (2nd ed., pp. 177–184). Washington, DC: Society for the Teaching of Psychology. Retrieved from http://teachpsych.org/Resources/Documents/ebooks/pnpp2014.pdf

Twombly, S. B. (2004). Looking for signs of community college arts and sciences faculty professionalization in searches: An alternative approach to a vexing question. *Community College Review, 32*, 21–39. http://dx.doi.org/10.1177/009155210403200102

Twombly, S. B. (2005). Values, policies, and practices affecting the hiring process for full-time arts and sciences faculty in community colleges. *The Journal of Higher Education, 76*, 423–447. http://dx.doi.org/10.1353/jhe.2005.0032

Twombly, S. B., & Townsend, B. K. (2008). Community college faculty: What we know and need to know. *Community College Review, 36*, 5–24. http://dx.doi.org/10.1177/0091552108319538

Vazin, T. (2014). The successful job applicant at Alabama State University. In J. N. Busler, B. C. Beins, & W. Buskist (Eds.), *Preparing the new psychology professoriate: Helping graduate students become competent teachers* (2nd ed., pp. 144–147). Washington, DC: Society for the Teaching of Psychology. Retrieved from http://teachpsych.org/Resources/Documents/ebooks/pnpp2014.pdf

Vick, J. M., Furlong, J. S., & Lurie, R. (2016). *The academic job search handbook* (5th ed.). Philadelphia: University of Pennsylvania Press. http://dx.doi.org/10.9783/9780812292060

Wells, T. T., Schofield, C. A., Clerkin, E. M., & Sheets, E. S. (2013). The academic job market: Advice from the front lines. *The Behavior Therapist, 36*, 39–49.

Wicherski, M., Michalski, D., & Kohout, J. (2009). *2007: Doctorate employment survey*. Washington, DC: American Psychological Association. Retrieved from http://www.apa.org/workforce/publications/07-doc-empl/index.aspx?tab=1

Woody, W. D., & Alcorn, M. B. (2014). Seeking a teacher-scholar in the School of Psychological Sciences at the University of Northern Colorado. In J. N. Busler, B. C. Beins, & W. Buskist (Eds.), *Preparing the new psychology professoriate: Helping graduate students become competent teachers* (2nd ed., pp. 148–153). Washington, DC: Society for the Teaching of Psychology. Retrieved from http://teachpsych.org/Resources/Documents/ebooks/pnpp2014.pdf

Wright, M. C., Kain, E. L., Kramer, L., Howery, C. B., Assar, N., McKinney, K., . . . Atkinson, M. (2004). Greedy institutions: The importance of institutional context for teaching in higher education. *Teaching Sociology, 32*, 144–159. http://dx.doi.org/10.1177/0092055X0403200201

Youn, T. I. K., & Price, T. M. (2009). Learning from the experience of others: The evolution of faculty tenure and promotion rules in comprehensive institutions. *The Journal of Higher Education, 80*, 204–237. http://dx.doi.org/10.1080/00221546.2009.11772139

Index

About the Author

Guy A. Boysen, PhD, is a professor of psychology at McKendree University. He received his bachelor's degree from Saint John's University in Collegeville, Minnesota, and his PhD from Iowa State University in Ames, Iowa. His scholarship emphasizes the teaching of psychology, professional development of teachers, and stigma of mental illness. He previously coauthored a book on model teaching characteristics titled *An Evidence-Based Guide to College and University Teaching*. Dr. Boysen's scholarship has led to consulting editor appointments with the journals *Teaching of Psychology* and *Scholarship of Teaching and Learning in Psychology*.